Published by Greenways Publishing Ltd
Tuition House
St George's Road
Wimbledon
SW19 4EU

© Greenways Publishing 2016

ISBN: 978-1-78281-766-6

Editor: David Emery
Designer: David Shad

Contributors:
James Lawton, Patrick Collins, Steve Curry, John Keith, Bob Harris, Stuart Hammonds,
John Lyons, Sam Elliott, Matt Badcock, Sam Jackson,
Hugo Varley, Jack Roberts, Matthew David

Printed by:
NEOGRAFIA
Sucianska 39A
038 61 Martin-Priekopa
Slovakia

Illustrations:
Bob Bond

1966 AND ALL THAT!

THE 50TH ANNIVERSARY

WELCOME

It was West Germany manager Helmut Schoen who summed up our World Cup winning team as well as anyone. "They are a side with ball winners and ball players," he said. He was right, we were a great combination, a team without egos, willing to work for each other.

Our defence was formidable with Gordon Banks, the best goalkeeper I ever played with behind myself and the super skilful Ray Wilson at full-back. Both Ray and I had pace. I was a champion 100-200 yard sprinter and we could both outrun our opposition wingers.

Between us we had big Jack Charlton. If it was in the air he got his head to it. I loved playing alongside him, he was utterly reliable, so effective and far better than some of his critics suggested.

Then there was Bobby Moore breaking up attacks with that marvellous intuition and pinging balls into the channels for the tireless Roger Hunt and later the powerful Geoff Hurst to chase down with their cross-over runs. And Bobby Charlton to smash them in from anywhere.

Ray and I both knew that if we were were drawn upfield and out of position Alan Ball and Martin Peters would be back filling in the gaps and, of course, Nobby was busy crunching the opposition.

And we had Alf. He was the glue which held us all together. We believed in Alf. We believed in his tactics, his team selection. We knew he believed in us and would back us.

So it proved. Nobby flattened the French captain with a late challenge. "Why did you do that, Nobby?" I asked him. "He called me Norbert," rasped Nobby.

The FA wanted Alf to drop Nobby. Drop him and I walk away said Alf who had agreed to take on the England job only under the strict understanding that he had complete control of team affairs. Nobby played on, shackled the great Eusebio in the semi and we were in the final against West Germany.

As extra time loomed against the Germans, Alf came onto the pitch in the interval. "Don't sit down," he ordered. "Don't roll down your socks, tuck in your shirts. Look at the Germans."

They were almost spread-eagled on the pitch with exhaustion. We knew then we would win. Hurst scored his great hat-trick as Jimmy Greaves watched from the bench. I had played with Jimmy since we were London schoolboys together. I felt for him.

But it was like all sport, all tournaments. There is good luck and bad luck running through them. Jimmy had bad luck. He had lost a little form, to be honest, going into the tournament after a dose of jaundice. That mercurial snap inside the box had dimmed. Then he was injured against the French and in came Hurst, as good a header of the ball as Tommy Lawton.

With Hunt he made the perfect combination. Alf was right to persevere with him even when Jimmy was declared fit for the final. It was Jimmy's bad luck, but it was Geoff's good luck. And, ultimately ours.

George Cohen MBE

ENGLAND SWINGS

BY DAVID EMERY
former head of sport
Express Newspapers

I t was the era of The Beatles, Twiggy, Carnaby Street and James Bond. The Swinging Sixties with its E-Type Jaguars and mini-skirts, Simon Dee on TV and Radio Caroline transmitting on a pirate wave band from Felixstowe.

Daily newspapers like the Daily Express and Daily Mirror were battling to breach the magical circulation figure of five million a day...and the nation, intoxicated by the new freedoms and sense of vibrance that washed technicolour images over the grey drabness of the post war years, hungered for modern heroes in music, cinema...and sport.

By 1964 a 17-year-old George Best had made his debut for Manchester United and Leeds had been promoted from the Second Division to begin their battle for supremacy with Liverpool.

The old guard changed. Danny Blanchflower, double winning captain of Tottenham Hotspur, retired at 38, passing on his vision for The Glory Game to younger men.

By 1965 Liverpool had won the FA Cup for the first time in their history... and Alf Ramsey was watching his England team develop into a mighty force.

Ramsey, the former England full-back and captain, had been appointed in 1963 and promptly informed the

E-Type Jaguar

public that England would win the 1966 World Cup under his new captain, the 22-year-old Bobby Moore.

A few months later, after a 5-2 defeat by France had knocked Ramsey's men out of the European Championships, that prediction looked a little suspect. But by 1965 Ramsey's team were in their stride.

The new manager had ensured that he had full power over selection of his team, a privilege not extended to his illustrious predecessor Walter Winterbottom. With the nucleus of the squad that would be victorious a year later, defeats of Hungary, West Germany, Sweden and Spain plus draws with Scotland, Yugoslavia and Wales showed welcome signs of improvement.

The start of World Cup year itself was a revelation as England stormed to victories over West Germany, Scotland, Yugoslavia, Finland, Norway and Denmark.

Now the great test was upon them. Sales of black and white televisions boomed, a nation waited...

The Beatles

LIKE A PENDULUM

Twiggy, the face of fashion

Sean Connery as James Bond

Carnaby Street

Danny Blanchflower

Dog called Pickles gets the FA out of a major stew

BY SAM JACKSON

Before the Championship started there was one major drama in store...the World Cup itself had gone missing. The gleaming Jules Rimet trophy, made from solid gold was stolen on 20 March 1966 from the Methodist Central Hall in Westminster where it was being exhibited in a glass cabinet.

It was found two weeks later on a London Street, remarkably by a mongrel dog called Pickles, who became an overnight sensation, appearing in feature films and commercials.

The amazing episode was told on the Channel 4 programme *Who Stole the Cup* and brilliantly put together by the *Observer's* Jamie Jackson.

For the Football Association and Sir Stanley Rous, the English president of FIFA, the theft was a nightmare scenario. Three months before hosting the 1966 World Cup, there was no trophy.

Before the theft became public, the FA secretary, Denis Follows, visited silversmith George Bird at his workshop in Fenchurch Street. Follows asked Bird to make a replica of the trophy from the same solid gold as the original, and was told nothing else other than to keep his mouth shut. Very few people, including Rous, knew about the visit.

The investigation was handed over to the Flying Squad's top man, DI Len Buggy. His break came when the Chelsea and FA chairman Joe Mears was phoned by a man calling himself Jackson. "There will be a parcel at Chelsea Football Club tomorrow. Follow the instructions inside," he told Mears.

On the Wednesday after the theft, the packet arrived containing part of the Jules Rimet trophy. A ransom note demanded £15,000 in five and one pound notes.

Where's the World Cup? The empty display case

"Dear Joe Kno (sic) no doubt you view with very much concern the loss of the World Cup..." it began. "To me it is only so much scrap gold. If I don't hear from you by Thursday or Friday at the latest I assume it's one for the POT."

Jackson called, seeking confirmation that Mears had the parcel. "Give me £15,000 on Friday and the cup will arrive by cab on Saturday," he said.

As Jackson requested, Mears posted the message, "Willing to do business Joe," in Thursday's edition of London's *Evening News*. But he ignored the warning not to tell the police.

On Friday, Buggy arrived at Mears' home but the FA chairman, an angina sufferer, had to go to bed because of stress. So Buggy arranged with Mrs Mears that he would pose as her husband's assistant 'McPhee' when Jackson called.

After some hesitation, Jackson agreed to a rendezvous in Battersea Park. Buggy arrived in Mears' fawn Ford Zodiac with £500 in bundles and the

CONTINUED >>

Pickles with owner David Corbett and his wife Jeanne

remainder of the ransom made from newspaper.

He was told to drive around south London for ten minutes, before he and Jackson turned off Kennington Park Road. Now, though, the operation went wrong and history opened its door to Pickles. Jackson saw a Transit van and guessed correctly that it was Buggy's back-up team. He tried to escape, but was arrested.

The thief's real name was Edward Betchley, a 46-year-old former soldier who had served in the Royal Armoured Corps during the Second World War in Egypt and Italy, before being demobbed with an 'exemplary character' in January, 1946.

With a previous conviction in 1954 for receiving tins of corned beef, Betchley was hardly bigtime. And at Rochester Row police station, he insisted that he was just the middleman, paid £500 for his part. All Betchley added was that the man behind the theft was known as The Pole. It is not clear if he actually existed.

Enter Pickles.

Seven days after Bletchley's court case David Corbett left his ground-floor flat in Norwood, south London with Pickles, the four-year-old mongrel he had taken off his brother John's hands, when he was a puppy, because he chewed furniture.

Pickles started sniffing around at the bottom of a suburban garden hedge in Beulah Hill.

Corbett recalled: "Pickles drew my attention to a package, tightly bound in newspaper. I picked it up and tore some paper away and saw a woman holding a dish over her head, and disks with the words Germany, Uruguay, Brazil.

"I rushed inside to my wife. She was one of those anti-sport wives. But I said, 'I've found the World Cup!

Pickles and his new-found fame

I've found the World Cup!'"

The media attention was worldwide.

Corbett recalled: "The general election was due but this knocked Harold Wilson off the front pages. When my mates realised they said, "Bloody hell. I bet you nicked it!" Corbett was indeed originally a suspect but was eventually cleared.

Pickles began the life of a celebrity. He starred in a feature film, *The Spy with the Cold Nose*, with Eric Sykes and June Whitfield and appeared on *Blue Peter* and many other TV shows. He was made Dog of the Year and awarded a year's free supply of food from Spillers.

At a party on the evening of England's 4-2 victory over West

Germany in the final, Pickles was picked up by Bobby Charlton on the balcony of their hotel in Kensington as the players greeted the cheering crowds below.

Mears died on 1 July, 1966 from the angina attack brought on by the theft, while Betchley, having served the two-year sentence he received for demanding money with menaces, died in 1969 of emphysema.

Pickles' luck also ran out the year after his great find. 'My six-year-old had him on a choke lead,' recalls Corbett. 'He shot after a cat and pulled my son over, before disappearing. I looked for over an hour. Then, in the gardens behind my house I saw him up on a tree. His chain was around the branch. Pickles just hung there.'

Corbett buried him in the back garden of the house in Lingfield, Surrey, that his £3,000 reward money had bought.

BY JAMES LAWTON
Sports Writer of the Year
Daily Express
Sports Columnist of the Year
The Independent

Bobby Moore and Alan Ball having gone, you might say the heroic team that made the finest, most uplifting day in the history of English football has lost both its head and its heart. However, it is also true that some legacies are proofed against all the cruelties of time.

Something else is self-evident 50 years after Moore wiped the sweat from his hands to receive the World Cup from the charmed young Queen, and the glowing whippersnapper Ball panted in his wake, and Nobby Stiles danced his joyful jig and the Charlton brothers,

The manager, the soon to be knighted Alf Ramsey, had always said that his challenge was not to fine tune the most gifted players in the land – and if you doubted this you had only to look at the ambivalent expression of the great striker Jimmy Greaves who had been condemned to the bench – but find a common thread of effort and commitment, an understanding that as never before in their careers they were only as good as the men who stood by their side.

At the funeral of this shamefully neglected man in the parish church of Ipswich, where he retired with the knighthood awarded in the first flush of national celebration - and a pitiful pension from the Football Association – two of his players, George Cohen, the quintessential Ramsey foot soldier and the knighted Bobby Charlton, delivered eulogies of a remarkable unanimity. They agreed that the gift of Ramsey was

DIAMOND DAY DAZZLE US FOR

who had had their family battles, embraced on the field and agreed that they had a moment they would cherish for as long as they lived.

It is that in the end you simply could not separate one individual achievement from another.

This is not because of any blurring of memory. It is a re-affirmation of a reality which every surviving member of the team insists will be prized highest in all their recall of the football life.

The truth, they will always say, is that they were in receipt of the greatest gift any competitor, any fighter, can take into action. It is one of certainty, not only in themselves but those around them.

Yes, uniquely, it was a day of supreme English sports heroes, men who found the strength of character and all the facility of their talent when they needed it most but when the final whistle was blown there was an extraordinary reaching out from each one of them to the quirky, sometimes infuriating figure who in the moment of his greatest triumph made clear his intention of remaining in the shadows.

the means to beat the world, a time in their lives when the road ahead was so acutely mapped it might have been the result of military radar.

A decade later Charlton remembered both the warmth and the intensity of the occasion. He concluded the volume devoted to his England days thus, "You may have noticed that all the roads I have travelled as an England player have led me forward or back to Sir Alf Ramsey. There is a good reason for this because, for me, he will always be the heart of English football that still beats down the years. He gave it strength and purpose and led it back into the wide world of the international game.

"If the lessons he taught are ignored it is, I still believe so long after his triumph, to the detriment of the English team. Even more saddening for me than his failure to qualify for the 1974 World Cup was the way he was allowed to leave, without significant honour or influence, to live with his ultimately fading memories.

"When his team gathered in the church to mourn his death on a bright spring morning in 1999 I was asked, with George Cohen, to speak. I told a few of the old stories of a tough and intransigent man and I got a few laughs but what I most wanted to say, in the best way I could, was that I would never stop being grateful for who he was and what he did.

"He knew football and he knew men. What he did, for me and my team-mates, was enable us to beat all of our fears and our doubts – and the world."

Charlton describes the occasion when that ambition which has seemed as much an unlikely fantasy as a piece of history down all the ensuing years of under-achievement, and sometimes abject failure, was seized as the 'diamond of his days'.

BOBBY CHARLTON

WILL EVER

It was a day of fleeting sunshine and sporadic rain showers, a day of huge promise and some haunting fears, and when it was over, when London and the country had a party said to rival the one that erupted on the night of Victory in Europe 21 years earlier, the light and the sparkle of it, everyone knew, would last a life-time.

Yet, heaven knows, it was a jewel that had taken much hard and even painful polishing.

At first the doubts were widespread and profound. They threatened to invade the certainties of Ramsey, who earlier in his reign had gathered his players together and in his stilted, elocution-honed tones, declared, "Most certainly, gentlemen, we will win the World Cup." That was hardly the consensus when on the first day of the tournament England laboured to a goalless draw against the legendary defensive proficiency and cynicism of the twice world champions

ROGER HUNT

GEOFF HURST

GORDON BANKS

Uruguay. It seemed like the confirmation of the bleak diagnosis of the nation's number one pundit, Jimmy Hill, who had announced, "We won't win anything with this lot."

Yet Ramsey was monumentally unfazed. He re-assured his players that with remaining group games against Mexico and France, the Uruguayan impasse would be swept away, and meanwhile they would enjoy, the old movie buff announced delightedly, the hospitality of Sean Connery and the James Bond film company at Pinewood Studios. Connery said he was appalled by the treatment England had received from the media and Ramsey was said to have been charmed, for the only time in his life, by a Scottish accent.

Ramsey was right, of course, and it was as he would prove to be in all his essential reading of a World Cup that right from the start was invaded by extraordinary levels of intrigue and drama and, less upliftingly, some passages of quite wanton brutality.

Stunningly, it was the North Koreans who stole the first act. They arrived as a mysterious force and eventually retreated into their nation's stone-age political history – but not before they captured the imagination of the football world. They qualified for the quarter finals at the expense of the mighty Italy, whose players were bombarded with abuse and bad eggs when they arrived home at Genoa airport with their jackets over their heads.

Then, the story became scarcely believable. The Koreans swept to a 3-0 lead in the quarter final at Goodison Park, harassing Portugal, the team Ramsey most feared for their strength, their high level of skill and the phenomenal Eusebio, in the manner of some crack commando unit. Where,

CONTINUED >>

GROUP 1	GROUP 3
ENGLAND	BRAZIL
FRANCE	BULGARIA
MEXICO	HUNGARY
URUGUAY	PORTUGAL

GROUP 2	GROUP 4
ARGENTINA	ITALY
SPAIN	CHILE
SWITZERLAND	NORTH KOREA
WEST GERMANY	SOVIET UNION

LONDON, WEMBLEY
CAPACITY: 98,600

BIRMINGHAM, VILLA PARK
CAPACITY: 52,000

LONDON, WHITE CITY
CAPACITY: 76,567

LIVERPOOL, GOODISON PARK
CAPACITY: 50,151

precisely, had the Koreans come from?

There were few hints but one of them came from a former Manchester United youth player Stan Ackerly, who had played for the Australian team which faced the Koreans in a vast Asian and Oceanic qualifying group reduced to the two of them after a mass protest against FIFA politics.

Ackerly had watched his opponents training before dawn in the Korean countryside beyond his hotel. Memorably, he described them as 'six o'clock shadows' in their strange, almost ghostly menace. They were flesh-and-blood enough, however, when Pak Doo-Ik, the least heralded hero in the history of big-time football drilled in the 41st minute goal which sent the Italians home to only the warm embrace of their mothers and separated the manager Dr Edmundo Fabbri from his lucrative contract.

The Koreans swarmed past a most formidable Portuguese defence. Only the stupendous, four-goal response of Eusebio, reaching into the Korean net after scoring in his urgency, restored some calm in the storm.

But if Portugal had regained their status as England's most dangerous European rivals, if they had imposed some of the old order, they inevitably created an equivocal reaction to their progress. They had, after all, already contributed to the shackling of the world's most beloved team, the Brazilian world champions of 1958 and 1962, in a 3-1 group game victory disfigured by a sickening double tackle on the great Pele by veteran defender Joao Morais. Pele hobbled out of the tournament he had thrilled as a teenager eight years earlier in Sweden and would dazzle once

more in 1970, vowing never to compete in the World Cup again. It was an unfulfilled threat but his departure from the English stage incited rage in South America hugely augmented by Ramsey's description of Antonio Rattin's Argentina as 'animals' after the bitter, soulless animosity of England's quarter final victory.

Rattin, who quixotically but successfully sought the friendship of Bobby Charlton in later years, was dismissed – according to the German referee for, apart from anything else, 'the look in his eyes" – and his excruciatingly slow departure from the field provided one of the most poignant images of the game, a wistful fingering of the corner flag on the way to football oblivion.

By now there was a growing belief that England might indeed go the distance. It was a time of gathering angst for the slightly injured but essentially discarded super striker Jimmy Greaves, who was heard to hum the tune of 'What's it all about, Alfie", when it became clear that Ramsey was leaning in favour of the physically commanding and direct Geoff Hurst of West Ham and the honest industry of Liverpool's Roger Hunt.

Elsewhere in the dressing room, though, there was that growing conviction that Ramsey would find a way to win, a way which he had fashioned from all his experience as an England full-back, and not least the trauma of Hungary's astonishing triumph at Wembley in 1953, which shook the world if not the complacent foundations of the Football Association.

Bobby Charlton, one of the most unquestioning of Ramsey's disciples, found the perfect opportunity to

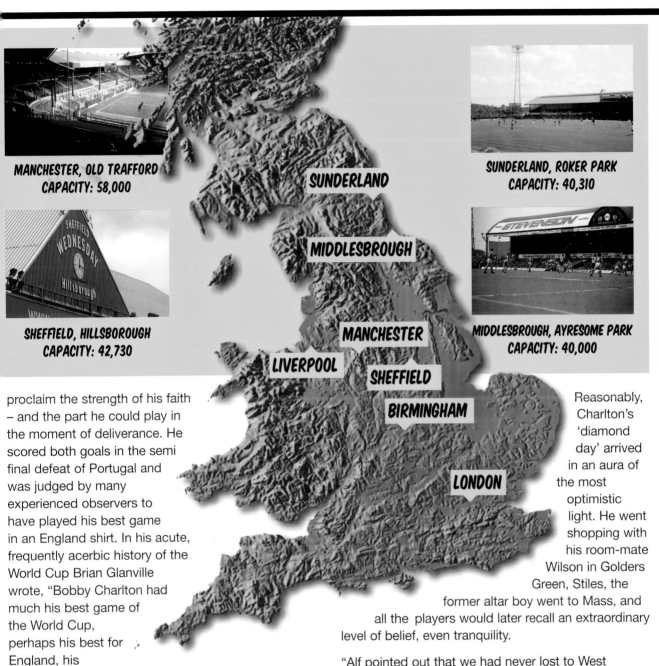

MANCHESTER, OLD TRAFFORD
CAPACITY: 58,000

SHEFFIELD, HILLSBOROUGH
CAPACITY: 42,730

SUNDERLAND, ROKER PARK
CAPACITY: 40,310

MIDDLESBROUGH, AYRESOME PARK
CAPACITY: 40,000

SUNDERLAND

MIDDLESBROUGH

MANCHESTER

LIVERPOOL

SHEFFIELD

BIRMINGHAM

LONDON

proclaim the strength of his faith – and the part he could play in the moment of deliverance. He scored both goals in the semi final defeat of Portugal and was judged by many experienced observers to have played his best game in an England shirt. In his acute, frequently acerbic history of the World Cup Brian Glanville wrote, "Bobby Charlton had much his best game of the World Cup, perhaps his best for England, his distribution for once being quite the equal of his fine running and shooting."

But then if Charlton was the shooting star, he was just part of a firmament that had never shone so brightly. Eusebio, who was supposed to eventually own this World Cup fought against the dying light as fiercely as he had against North Korea but the Koreans didn't have Nobby Stiles.

Eusebio thundered home another penalty near the end but he left the field with tears of frustration rolling down his broad and engaging face. Stiles had been an unshakeable limpet. Bobby Moore had been imperious, Alan Ball insatiable in his running, Martin Peters knowing and sharp, Hurst and Hunt relentless, Cohen and Wilson and Jack Charlton quite tigerish in their application, and Gordon Banks was on the point of establishing himself as the world's best goalkeeper.

Reasonably, Charlton's 'diamond day' arrived in an aura of the most optimistic light. He went shopping with his room-mate Wilson in Golders Green, Stiles, the former altar boy went to Mass, and all the players would later recall an extraordinary level of belief, even tranquility.

"Alf pointed out that we had never lost to West Germany and there was no earthly reason why we should begin now," George Cohen recalls.

An early goal from Helmut Haller, after a rare error from the normally immaculate Ray Wilson and, potentially more devastating, an equaliser from Wolfgang Weber in the last seconds of full time, challenged this blithe assumption, but only fleetingly. Hurst scored his unique World Cup final hat-trick, his final goal a last thunderous interring of the controversy over his second which the Germans still insist did not cross the line, and there was Moore the young, blond emperor claiming his and his team-mates' dues.

And what, precisely, were they? They were the statements of a belief that English football, all these years on, still yearns to find again. The certainty, that is, of believing that you have the means to be the best in the world.

THE WINNERS...

WHERE ARE

WHAT CAME NEX

THE REST OF THE SQUAD...

THEY NOW?

OR THE HEROES OF WEMBLEY?

1. SIR ALF RAMSEY (Born January 22 1920, Sheffield – Died April 28 1999)

Ramsey managed England from 1963 to 1974 and was knighted in 1967 in recognition of England's World Cup win. He also led England to third place in the 1968 European Championship and the quarter-finals of the 1970 World Cup and the 1972 European Championship. As a player, Ramsey was a full-back with Tottenham and a member of England's 1950 World Cup squad. In all he won 32 caps and captained the side three times. His grasp of tactics earned him the nickname 'The General'. Ramsey retired from playing in 1955 to become manager of Ipswich Town, then in the third tier of English football. Ipswich rose through the divisions and become champions of England in 1962. Ramsey managed Birmingham City during the 1977–78 season, then acted as an advisor at Greek club Panathinaikos in 1979–80. He died in Ipswich in 1999, aged 79, and a statue in his honour was built outside Ipswich's home ground at Portman Road.

2. GEORGE COHEN MBE
(Born October 22 1939, Kensington)

Right full-back Cohen was a one-club man, spending 14 years with Fulham and playing 459 games before moving into coaching with them. He won 37 caps for England after taking over the role from Jimmy Armfield. Cohen was diagnosed with bowel cancer in the mid-80s but beat the disease after a 14-year battle. Tottenham Hotspur bid £82,000 to sign Cohen from Fulham soon after they had acquired another Fuham great, Alan Mullery. But the then Fulham chairman, Tommy Trinder, turned it down. George is the uncle of 2003 Rugby World Cup winner Ben Cohen.

3. NOBBY STILES MBE
(Born May 18 1942, Manchester)

The least-capped member of the '66 team with 28 famously danced with trophy at Wembley. Nobby claimed the European Cup with Manchester United as well as two FA Cups and a League title. He moved to Middlesbrough and Preston before retiring in 1975. He managed Preston, Vancouver Whitecaps and West Bromwich Albin before going into coaching with Man Utd, where he was involved with the youth squads that developed the 'Class of '92'. Nobby had a stroke in 2010, followed by a diagnoses of prostate cancer in 2014 and is now battling Alzheimer's.

4. JOHN 'JACK' CHARLTON OBE
(Born May 8 1935, Ashington)

Jack Charlton, the older brother of Bobby Charlton, played club football solely for Leeds, amassing 629 appearances (still a club record) and 70 goals as an old-fashioned centre-half. He made his England debut in 1965 and won 35 caps. Jack then went on to managerial success with Middlesbrough and Sheffield Wednesday, securing promotion with both teams. He then took charge of the Republic of Ireland leading them to their first World Cup in 1990 and again in '94. He retired in 1996.

5. GORDON BANKS OBE
(Born December 30 1937, Sheffield)

England's number one amassed 73 caps for his country and is renowned for the 'save of the century' from Pele in 1970. He was named FIFA goalkeeper of the year six times. In '72, the year he helped Stoke win the League Cup and was named Fooballer of the Year, he lost the sight of his right eye in a car crash. That ended his professional career although he did make 37 appearances for Ford Lauderdale Strikers in the USA between 1977-78. Banks briefly managed Telford United. Now president of Stoke, a statue has been erected to him at the Britannia Stadium. He lost a kidney to cancer in 2006 and revealed in December 2015 that he was again fighting the disease.

6. RAY WILSON MBE
(Born December 17 1934, Shirebrook)

The left-back won 63 caps for England during a playing career which spanned Huddersfield Town, Everton, Oldham Athletic and Bradford City. Wilson became an apprentice railwayman on leaving school but was spotted playing amateur football by a scout at Huddersfield. Quickly singled out as a strong and nippy left back with good overlapping skills by the then Huddersfield Town manager Bill Shankly. Retired from football in '71 after a serious knee injury, Wilson resided in Halifax and became an undertaker. After 26 years in that line of work he retired fully and in. Sold his World Cup medal in 2002 for £70,000 to fund his retirement with his wife in Huddersfield.

7. ALAN BALL MBE
(Born May 12 1945, Farnworth – Died April 25 2007)

The 'lad' of the team at just 21, midfielder Ball's all-action performance at '66 was rewarded with a then record £110,000 move from Blackpool to Everton, which culminated in winning the League in 1970. He later moved to Arsenal for a record £220,000. His illustrious 23 year career saw over 800 games played for Blackpool, Everton, Arsenal, Southampton and Bristol Rovers. In 1980 he moved into management and spent 14 years with Blackpool, Portsmouth, Stoke, Exeter, Southampton and Manchester City. He retired

from the game in 1999 to care for his wife Lesley before she passed away in 2004 from ovarian cancer. Alan died from a heart attack while battling a blaze in his garden in 2007.

8. SIR GEOFF HURST
(Born December 8 1941, Ashton-under-Lyne)

Grew in stature throughout the tournament when he replaced the injured Jimmy Greaves and scored that memorable hat-trick in the Final. A powerful centre-forward, Hurst made 411 appearances for West Ham (180 goals) and 108 starts for Stoke City (30 goals). He managed Telford United and Chelsea and had a five year spell as England assistant manager to Ron Greenwood before he joined Martin Peters in the insurance business. He now resides with wife Judith in Cheltenham. He was knighted in 1998. Hurst sold his 1966 shirt at auction in 2000 for £91,750. It has since been valued at £2.3m.

9. SIR BOBBY CHARLTON
(Born October 11 1937, Ashington)

The name is synonymous with football throughout the world. The flying winger with the cannonball shot became England's great central midfield player under Alf Ramsey. His legend grew when he survived the Munich Air Disaster and then scored two goals against Benfica as Manchester United won the European Cup in 1968. Until overtaken by Wayne Rooney last year he was England's all-time leading goal-scorer with 49 from 108 appearances. Following his playing career he spent two years as manager of Preston before being appointed to the Manchester United board in 1984. Knighted in 1994, Sir Bobby still holds an active role at Old Trafford as an ambassador.

10. BOBBY MOORE OBE
(Born April 12 1941, Barking – Died February 24 1993)

Essex-born England legend Bobby Moore captained the side to World Cup glory. The original Golden Boy captained West Ham United and was cited by Pele as the greatest defender he had ever played against. Moore won a total of 108 caps for England, which at the time of his international retirement in 1973 was a national record. He made 544 appearances for West Ham before moving to Fulham and guiding them to the 1974 FA Cup Final against West Ham. Fulham lost 2-0.

CONTINUED >>

Following his career he was appointed Sports Editor for Sunday Sport in 1988 followed by a role as sports analyst for Capital Gold in 1990. Bobby was diagnosed with bowel cancer in '91 and died on February 24 1993. The Bobby Moore Fund provides support for those suffering from similar diseases.

11. ROGER HUNT MBE
(Born July 20 1938, Glazebury)

One of the first names on Alf Ramsey's team sheet, the tireless, selfless Hunt was the workhorse who helped first Jimmy Greaves and then Geoff Hurst achieve their goal-scoring magic. Not that the Liverpool forward was any slouch in front of goal himself. In 34 England appearances, he scored 18 goals. In 404 League appearances for Liverpool he hit 245 club goals and on 22 August 1964, he scored against Arsenal after 11 minutes in a 3–2 home win, the first ever goal seen on the BBC's Match of the Day. Hunt later played for Bolton Wanderers, 24 goals in 76 appearances, before retiring in 1972 and to work for his family haulage business in Warrington.

12. MARTIN PETERS MBE
(Born November 8 1943, Plaistow)

The midfielder who was described by Alf Ramsey as 'being ten years ahead of his time' put England 2-1 up in the World Cup Final. In all he scored 20 England goals in 67 appearances. His League career spanned West Ham Tottenham, Norwich and Sheffield United in 721 matches which brought 174 goals. Following retirement in 1981 he became Sheffield Utd manager before he and good friend Geoff Hurst left the game to go into business together with 'MotorPlan' which specialised in car insurance in Essex. Following this, Peters became a non-executive director at Spurs in which he advised on footballing matters as well as acting as a match day host.

13. PETER BONETTI
(Born September 27 1941, Putney)

Third goalkeer Peter Bonetti claimed seven England caps in his career that is most remembered for the blunders against West Germany in the quarter final of the 1970 World Cup after Banks had succumbed to food poisoning. Still, he is widely regarded as one of the greatest goalkeepers to play for Chelsea for whom he made 600 apearances over two spells. A final flourish of five games for Dundee in '70 coincided with his running of a guesthouse on the Isle of Mull and a stint as a postman. After retiring in '79 Bonetti took to coaching with spells at Chelsea, Manchester City and the England national side.

14. RON SPRINGETT
(Born July 22 1935, Fulham – Died September 12 2015)

Back-up goalkeeper to Gordon Banks, Springett debuted for England in '59 and represented the nation at two World Cups – '62 & '66 in his 33 caps. He amassed 384 appearances for Sheffield Wednesday and a further 147 for QPR in two spells. On retirement in 1969 he opened a sports shop on Uxbridge Road near Loftus Road. Selling his business after three years, Springett turned to interior decorating to fund his retirement. He could be regularly seen at Loftus Road before passing away at the age of 80.

15. RON FLOWERS
(Born July 28 1934, Doncaster)

Ron spent the majority of his life in Wolverhampton, playing for Wanderers between 1951-1967 as an attacking half-back (modern midfielder) and making 457 appearances. He went on to finish his career at Northampton before opening a sports shop 'Ron Flowers Sport' which trades today in Wolverhampton, managed now by his sons. He made 49 appearances for England, including the 1962 World Cup, and scored ten goals.

16. JIMMY ARMFIELD CBE
(Born September 21 1935, Manchester)

The former England captain and full-back spent his entire career at Blackpool playing 627 gamed. His loyalty was rewarded with a bronze statue being constructed outside Bloomfield Road in 2001. He won 43 caps for England, 15 as captain. Played in the 1962 World Cup where he was acclaimed as the best right-back in the world. Jimmy moved into management, most notably with Bolton and Leeds, leading them into the European Cup final in 1975. Armfield then took up a post as Daily Express football correspondent in Manchester and currently works with Radio 5 Live as a pundit after beating non Hodgkin lymphoma in the early 2000's.

17. NORMAN HUNTER
(Born October 29 1943, Gateshead)

Norman 'Bites Yer Legs' Hunter is a Leeds legend who won six major honours with the club including two European trophies in his 540 appearances over 14 years. He later played for Bristol City. Renowned for his fierce tackling, the centre-back won 28 caps for England and it was even rumoured that Alf Ramsey had considered playing him in the Final against West Germany in place of Bobby Moore because of his tenacity. Following his playing career Hunter became manager of Barnsley, Rotherham and Leeds (caretaker). He also undertook local media work, and became an after-dinner speaker. Like other reserves, he received his World Cup medal in 2009.

18. JIMMY GREAVES
(Born February 20 1940, Manor Park)

Famously not selected for the '66 Final itself, Greaves was a goal-scorer supreme netting 44 from his 57 games with England. He had also scored 13 in 12 appearances for England Under 23. Greaves did not receive his World Cup medal until a change of FIFA rules in 2009. He mirrored his goal-scoring form at London clubs Chelsea (124 goals from 157 appearances) and Spurs (220 from 321). In between his stints at Chelsea and Spurs, Greaves was sold to AC Milan for £80,000 in April 1961. Despite scoring nine goals in 12 games he never settled and was sold to Spurs for £99,999 in December 1961. He later moved to West Ham, 38 games 13 goals. In August 1977 after declaring himself an alcoholic, Greaves made his debut for Barnet and went on to net 25 goals for them and was their player of the season. After retiring at the end of that season, Greaves embarked on a successful broadcasting career, including the Saint and Greavsie Show with Ian St John from 1985-1992. Greaves suffered a serious stroke in May 2015.

19. GERRY BYRNE
(Born August 29 1938 – Died November 28 2015)

A one-club hero for Liverpool with 264 appearances, the left-back famously played in the 1965 Cup Final with a broken collarbone as Liverpool beat Leeds 2-1 to win the Cup for the first time. He won two England caps. Byrne had joined Liverpool straight from school as a 15 year old and was offered a professional contract the day after his 17th birthday. When Bill Shankly was appointed manager in December 1959 he instigated a clear-out of 24 players. Notably Byrne and Roger Hunt were retained. Following his retirement from playing, Gerry took up coaching roles at the club. He died in a Wrexham nursing home after suffering from Alzheimers.

20. IAN CALLAGHAN MBE
(Born April 10 1942, Toxteth)

Four caps in 11 years for England, the Liverpool winger holds the record appearances for his club with 857 in all competitions, winning five League title, two FA Cups and two European Cups. He later played for Swansea and Crewe before retiring aged 39. He started an insurance sales business in Lydiate and can still be seen at Anfield as he is a regular as president of the Official Liverpool FC Fan club. Callaghan received his World Cup medal in 2009, becoming one of only three English footballers to have a World Cup and a European Cup winner's medal, following Manchester United's Bobby Charlton and Nobby Stiles.

21. TERRY PAINE MBE
(Born March 23 1939, Winchester)

Southampton's record League appearance holder with 713 games, Terry was named their 'honorary president' in 2012. He later played for Hereford United and helped them to the Third Division title before retiring in 1977. The winger played 19 times for England, scoring seven goals. He emigrated to South Africa and began to work closely with the country's Football Association as an ambassador and successfully aided the 2010 World Cup bid.

22. GEORGE EASTHAM CBE
(Born September 23 1936, Blackpool)

The skilful inside forward (midfielder) was part of a footballing family. His father George Eastham snr was an England international who played for Bolton and Blackpool while his uncle Harry Eastham played for Liverpool and Accrington Stanley. Eastham junior first played for Northern Irish club Ards where his father was player manager. Winning goal scorer in the1972 League Cup Final for Stoke, beating Chelsea 2-1, Eastham is most famously remembered for successfully battling against the 'retain and transfer' system which paved the way for the free movement of footballers. After a successful career with Newcastle, Arsenal and Stoke and 19 England caps, Eastham emigrated to South Africa. He set up his own sportswear business as well as being a football coach for local black children (being a noted opponent of Apartheid).

23. JOHN CONNELLY
(Born July 18 1938, St Helens – Died October 25 2012)

Played for Burnley, Manchester United, Blackburn and Bury as a winger. In the 1959–60 season, Connelly played a crucial part in helping Burnley win the League with 20 goals in 34 appearances. He won a second Championship medal with Manchester United in 1965. He won 20 England caps, scoring seven goals. Became 'Justice of Peace' for Reedley and opened a fish and chip shop named 'Connelly's Plaice' in the Lancashire Moors before dying peacefully at home aged 74.

ENGLAND 0 URUGUAY 0

BY MATTHEW DAVID

O h, England what a start! read the back page of the *Daily Express* as leading columnist Desmond Hackett lamented how England had laboured "against a light-blue brick wall of defiance called Uruguay" in the opening match of the World Cup in front of a packed, expectant Wembley.

"After the glories of the opening ceremony," wrote Hackett, "the first commandment of the World Cup was written starkly across the noble turf of Wembley: Thou shalt not lose."

Uruguay, a proud football nation who had twice won the World Cup, in 1930 and 1950, showed their deep respect for England by packing eight or nine men behind the ball each time Bobby Moore's team threatened to attack.

England huffed and puffed, ran endlessly and with endeavour, securing 15 corners in the process to Uruguay's one. But they could not get past the South American bus.

England were permitted only two shots that demanded saves and the first of those did not arrive until the 65th minute.

The Uruguayans were booed endlessly for their flagrant time-wasting, but the South American champions remained unhurried.

England flew into their rivals as Wembley roared raucous encouragement, but, slowly, the Uruguayans strangled the passion from the match.

Uruguay produced the first shot after 27 minutes when outside right Julio Crictes rifled in a shot that tested Gordon Banks.

Jimmy Greaves, who had a quiet night, fired England with a run and cross, but the inviting ball was missed by four players in white in the penalty area.

John Connolly broke free but the move came to nothing as England time and again found themselves like locksmiths confronted by a safe with a secret combination.

England never ceased to battle, showing spirit and courage. Jack Charlton crossed and Connolly missed by no more than six inches.

Manager Alf Ramsey remained defiant: "We will win this tournament," he said, repeating his prediction first made when he was appointed in 1963. "I was disappointed with the result but not with the performance. Uruguay were a good side. I was disappointed we didn't get a goal but with eight defenders in the 18 yard box we would have needed to be lucky to score.

"Everyone said we had an easy group after the draw was made. I told you different, and now you know. But we will still win."

BRAZIL 2 BULGARIA 0

Pele 13
Garrincha 63

BY MATT BADCOCK

Brazil began their quest for a hat-trick of World Cup wins with victory over Bulgaria courtesy of a free-kick each from Pele and Garrincha. The South Americans arrived in England as double world champions after lifting the trophy in Sweden in 1958 and in Chile four years later.

Just over 47,000 people crammed into Everton's Goodison Park to see the Samba stars and they weren't disappointed.

Pele, who was on the receiving end of some heavy tackles from the Bulgarian defenders, gave his side the lead in the 13th minute and became the first player to score in three successive World Cups.

After being fouled on the edge of the D, the 25-year-old dusted himself off to unleash a low shot that proved too powerful for keeper Georgi Naydenov to keep out.

But the CSKA Sofia keeper was equal to Jairzinho when he got down low to thwart the Brazilian following a wonderful attacking move shortly after.

Pele had been forced to miss the 1962 final against Czechoslovakia through injury; now he gave the fans everything they hoped for as he took on his opponents with dazzling skill.

A clever lob over the defence from the No.10 set Alcindo clear, only for Naydenov to once again keep the ball out.

Bulgaria had a good chance in the second half themselves. Brazil keeper Gilmar lost control of the ball but forward Georgi Asparuhov was unable to squeeze it in from a tight angle.

Brazil made them pay when Garrincha doubled the lead. The man known as the 'Bent-legged Angel' produced something from above by bending a glorious free-kick into the top corner.

Naydenov made another fantastic one-handed save to push away Pele's strike as Brazil went in search of a third. As it was, they had to settle for two and two points in their Group 3 opener.

WEST GERMANY 5 SWITZERLAND 0

Held 16, Haller 21, 77 (pen)
Beckenbauer 40, 52

T he imperious brilliance of Franz Beckenbauer and the all-round power of the West German football machine was unleashed on Switzerland in front of an awestruck Hillsborough. The 20-year-old Beckenbauer, playing on the right of midfield, twice drove through the heart of the Swiss defence with languid surges of power to score.

Anyone believing that England were favourites for the title would have had serious second thoughts after watching this magnificent exhibition of football. Siegfried Held opened the scoring after Uwe Seeler's 16th minute shot had rebounded from the post. Five minutes later Helmut Haller added the second, bursting clear from just over the halfway line to run on and beat goalkeeper Karl Elsener.

Beckenbauer began his command performance five minutes before half time when he raced forward and played a one-two with Uwe Seeler before sliding home his shot. The best was still to come from Der Kaiser seven minutes after half time as he strode through almost unopposed from the half-way line to add the third.

The Germans wrapped it up with a penalty after Seeler had been upended. Haller stroked home the spot kick with the Swiss protesting he had checked his run and unsettled the goalkeeper. Referee Hugh Phillips of Scotland was unmoved.

SOVIET UNION 3 NORTH KOREA 0

Malofeyev 31, 88
Banishevskiy 33

H eading into the 1966 finals as Asia's sole representative just over a decade after a war that had devastated and divided their country, North Korea were 1000-1 outsiders to win the World Cup, despite the proud boast of their specially composed World Cup anthem that proclaimed, "We can beat everyone, even the strongest team".

They had qualified by beating Australia in a playoff, after many other Asian and African countries had withdrawn in protest that only one team from the two continents would be granted a place in the finals.

Getting entry into the UK proved to be a challenge in itself for the North Koreans who lacked diplomatic relations with Great Britain since the Korean War. The British Foreign Office took their time granting the Koreans entry clearance, and relented only when it was agreed their national anthem would not be played before games.

The North Koreans entered the tournament as an enigma to the British Press. *The Times'* 1966 World Cup finals preview said that "the North Koreans, offering a string of names that have the sound of waterfalls, remain for the moment a mysterious, unknown quantity."

That shroud of mystery was lifted from the North Koreans in their first match, a 3-0 loss to the Soviet Union that earned them plaudits as plucky underdogs (or the "little Orientals", as *The Times* called them), who won the support of the Middlesbrough crowd.

The Soviets took control with a two-goal burst after half an hour, first through Eduard Malofeyev, then Anatoliy Banishevskiy. Malofeyev added the third two minutes from time.

The crowd politely clapped the Koreans, probably wondering what all the fuss was about. They were about to find out...

ELSEWHERE...

AT HILLSBOROUGH WEST GERMANY LOOKED VERY GOOD, ALTHOUGH SWITZERLAND WERE POOR. THEY PLAYED LIKE TOTAL STRANGERS, AS IF THEY HAD JUST BEEN DRAGGED RANDOMLY FROM THE CUCKOO CLOCK FACTORIES

IT'S THE WORLD CUP— YOU HAVE GOT SOME BOOTS?

YOU'VE PUT BOTH YOUR LEGS DOWN ONE KNICKER...

DOING THE OLD FASHIONED THINGS WELL, THE GERMANS PICKED THEM OFF AT REGULAR INTERVALS.

FRANZ BECKENBAUER IS SURE TO BE ONE OF THE STARS OF THIS TOURNAMENT.

THEY STOPPED AT FIVE-NIL. NIL WAS MORE THAN THE SWISS DESERVED.

WITHOUT BREAKING INTO A SWEAT, YOUNG BECKENBAUER SCORED TWICE FROM MIDFIELD WHILST ALSO DIRECTING HIS ELDERS WHAT TO DO.

AS SOON AS THEY SCORED I DIDN'T THINK IT WOULD END 0-0...

GERMANY'S LAST GOAL WAS A PENALTY.

ARE YOU SURE, REF?

RUSSIA BRUSHED ASIDE NORTH KOREA, WHO ARE ABSOLUTE NO-HOPERS. SO TINY THEY LOOKED LIKE SCHOOLBOYS... IF THEY GET OUT OF THIS GROUP, I'LL EAT MY PENCIL.

HUNGARY 1 PORTUGAL 3

Bene 59

Augusto 1, 65
Torres 89

BY JACK ROBERTS

For once, Eusebio was kept off the scoresheet, but Portugal showed they were far from a one-man band with a comprehensive defeat of the once mighty Magyars. In fact it took just one minute for Jose Augusto to put them ahead with the assistance of Benfica team-mate Antonio Simoes.

Hungary winger Ferenc Bene drew his side level in the 59th minute but parity was short lived as Jose Augusto, one of five Benfica players representing Portugal, fired his team back in front.

Eusebio did make a telling contribution a minute from time, setting up Jose Torres to complete a satisfying victory in front of 29,866 at Old Trafford.

The Black Pearl of Portugal, Eusebio

ITALY 2 CHILE 0

Mazzola 9
Barison 87

WHEN hosts Chile beat Italy 2-0 in a 1962 World Cup group match that became known as the Battle of Santiago, BBC sports commentator David Coleman described it as "the most stupid, appalling, disgusting and disgraceful exhibition of football, possibly in the history of the game".

So you could understand why the Italians were eager for revenge when the two sides met on European soil in a Group 4 clash four years later.

In front of a little over 27,000 spectators at Sunderland's Roker Park, Italy achieved their objective by reversing the scoreline from the previous World Cup when Chile went on to finish third.

Midfielder Sandro Mazzola put Italy ahead in the ninth minute, but it wasn't until Paolo Barison's 87th minute goal that the South Americans were finally killed off.

ARGENTINA 2 SPAIN 1

Artime 65, 79   Pirri 72

In the other Europe v South America clash on the same day, it was the latter who came out on top. Villa Park was the venue as Argentina got the better of Spain 2-1. With Group 2 seeds West Germany having demolished Switzerland 5-0 the previous day, it already looked as though it could be a pivotal match. Luis Artime gave Argentina the advantage in the 65th minute, but it seemed Spain would earn a point when Pirri levelled things up seven minutes later.

However, striker Artime bagged his second in the 79th minute – and this time there was no way back for the Spaniards.

FRANCE 1 MEXICO 1

Hausser 62   Borja 48

A match that England fans were keeping an eye on was the Group 1 encounter between France and Mexico. After the Three Lions' 0-0 disappointment against Uruguay in their opener, a draw between their other group rivals was probably the ideal outcome – and so it proved as the French and Mexicans played out a 1-1 draw at Wembley.

A crowd of almost 70,000 saw Mexico's 20-year-old striker Enrique Borja give his side the lead three minutes into the second half, but it was all-square just after the hour as Gerard Hausser struck for the French to leave the group delicately poised.

ELSEWHERE...

FRANCE, SPAIN AND ITALY ALL KICKED OFF LAST EVENING. IT'S HARD TO SEE ANY OF THEM BECOMING WORLD CHAMPIONS, NOT IN THE NEXT ONE HUNDRED YEARS. ALL HAVE FINE INDIVIDUALS, BUT MUST LEARN TO PLAY AS A TEAM.

TO YOU, GEORGE...

LIKE ENGLAND, WHO CAN SOMETIMES STRING TOGETHER **SIX** PASSES BEFORE A MOVE BREAKS DOWN.

BRILLIANT! I WISH I WAS WATCHING THIS FROM THE TERRACES...

SPAIN LOST TO ARGENTINA, FOR WHOM ARTIME TOOK HIS TWO GOALS ARTFULLY.

ANTONIO RATTIN STRODE ABOUT THE FIELD LIKE A COLOSSUS. WE SHALL SEE MORE OF ANTONIO, TO BE SURE...

WHEN ITALY MET CHILE IN 1962 IN SANTIAGO THEY KICKED GREAT LUMPS OUT OF EACH OTHER...

TASTE THE DUBBIN...

AT ROKER PARK LAST EVENING THEY AGREED THAT IT SHOULD BE ONLY THE BALL THAT WAS KICKED.

MAZZOLA, COMPLETE WITH MOUSTACHE, KICKED IT INTO CHILE'S NET, AND ITALY WON...

NICE...

MEXICO DREW WITH FRANCE, WHICH WAS AS GOOD AS A WIN TO THEIR FANS. BORJA, THEIR BIG STRIKER, LOOKS QUITE A HANDFUL. HIS GOAL WAS A REWARD FOR HIS PERSISTENCE.

ARE YOU WATCHING, ENGLAND? I'M COMING FOR YOU...

BRAZIL 1 HUNGARY 3

Tostao 14

Bene 2
Farkas 64
Meszoly (pen) 73

BY MATT BADCOCK

Hungary inflicted Brazil's first defeat in the World Cup since 1954 in a wonderful game packed with skill and flair. The Magyars were the last team to beat the current world champions when they triumphed 4-2 in the quarter-finals twelve years ago, before going on to lose the final to West Germany.

Brazil were without star forward Pele, who had picked up an injury following some rough treatment from defenders in their opening game against Bulgaria.

Hungary made the most of their opponents missing a vital player after just two minutes when 21-year-old Ferenc Bene sauntered into the box and fired past Gilmar from ten yards.

Brazil hit back just 12 minutes later when a loose ball fell to Tostao and he crashed in the equaliser.

They could have been ahead before half time had it not been for a last-gasp goal-line clearance by the Hungarian defence.

Having lost their first game to Portugal, Hungary were desperate for the win and they went back in front on 64 minutes.

A cross into the box from the right flank was met on the volley by Janos Farkas leaving Gilmar with no chance but to watch the ball fly past him into the bottom corner.

Hungary then made the game safe in the 73rd-minute. Bene was fouled in the box and English referee Ken Dagnall pointed to the penalty spot.

Kalman Meszoly made no mistake from 12 yards as he drilled the kick into the bottom corner leaving keeper Gilmar rooted to his line.

Florian Albert almost squeezed in a fourth from a narrow angle but it didn't matter with the Hungarians full value for their 3-1 win.

Brazil would have to hope talisman Pele was back for their third and final group game against Portugal, when it looked likely they would need a result to progress out of Group 3.

15TH JULY - AYRESOME PARK 13,792
CHILE 1 NORTH KOREA 1

Marcos (pen) 26   Pak Seung-Zin 88

NORTH Korea had been swatted aside 3-0 by the Soviet Union in their World Cup debut, so it was imperative they got something from their second Group 4 match against Chile. Chile also needed to bounce back after losing their opener to Italy and it appeared they would do so when they held the lead until the closing stages.

Midfielder Ruben Marcos had beaten teenage North Korean keeper Lee Chang Myung from the penalty spot in the 26th minute to give the South Americans the lead.

In front of a tournament low 13,792 crowd at Ayresome Park, Chile held their slender advantage until two minutes from time when North Korea captain Pak Seung-Zin rescued a precious point for his side to keep their World Cup dreams alive.

15TH JULY - WHITE CITY 45,662
URUGUAY 2 FRANCE 1

Rocha 27   De Bourgoing (pen) 15
Cortes 32

In England's group, Uruguay put themselves in a good position with a 2-1 victory against France. They had to do it the hard way at White City in front of a 45,662 crowd as the French opened the scoring on the quarter-hour mark, Hector De Bourgoing netting from the spot.

However, the Uruguayans were back level in the 27th minute through Pedro Rocha. Five minutes later they scored what turned out to be the winner courtesy of midfielder Julio Cortes.

15TH JULY - HILLSBOROUGH 32,028
SPAIN 2 SWITZERLAND 1

Sanchis 58   Quentin 29
Amancio 75

Spain and Switzerland had both lost their opening matches, adding pressure to their Group 2 showdown at Hillsborough. A crowd of just over 32,000 at the Sheffield venue saw Rene-Pierre Quentin give the Swiss the lead in the 29th minute and they held their advantage until half-time.

However, Spain fought back in the second half to take the spoils. Firstly, defender Manuel Sanchis scored the equaliser in the 58th minute. With 15 minutes left on the clock, striker Amancio became the Spanish hero by netting the winner - and left the Swiss pointless in the process.

ENGLAND 2 MEXICO 0

B Charlton 38
Hunt 75

BY JACK ROBERTS

Alf Ramsey's England scored their first goal and won their first match of the 1966 World Cup on this day. And what a goal it was! As against Uruguay in their opening Group 1 fixture, England again had to try and unlock an eight or nine-man defence.

This time it was provided by the plum-shirted Mexicans and there wasn't much to worry Calderon in Mexico's goal until a piece of magic from Bobby Charlton in the 38th minute.

Martin Peters intercepted a Mexican pass and moved the ball on to Roger Hunt. A quick pass inside gave Charlton possession just inside his own half and he ran free down the centre at pace.

He jinked left. Then right. Before firing a 25-yard screamer that flew into the top corner.

England's World Cup challenge was up and running.

With a quarter of an hour to go the stadium erupted again. Peters put Jimmy Greaves away with a perfect pass, Calderon could only palm his shot away and Hunt was in the right place to turn the ball in for 2-0.

Terry Paine, who was England's outside-right for the game, said of the strike: "Bobby Charlton's goal was the best England goal I ever saw."

PORTUGAL 3 BULGARIA 0

Vutsov og (17)
Eusebio 36
Torres 81

Portugal secured their second win of the tournament as they dispatched coach Rudolf Vytlail's Bulgaria in an entertaining game at Old Trafford. Portugal broke the deadlock midway through the first half in rather freak circumstances as Hungary's Ivan Vutsov headed past his own keeper despite being under little pressure from the Portuguese attackers.

Portugal's lead was doubled just before half time as Eusebio grabbed his first goal of the tournament. The striker hit an emphatic first time effort from ten yards past Hungary goalkeeper Georgi Naydenov.

The result was put beyond doubt with nine minutes remaining as Jose Torres capitalised on a slack bit of defending from Bulgaria captain Boris Gaganelov to slide the ball home for Portugal's third.

SOVIET UNION 1 ITALY 0

Chislenko 57

The Soviet Union secured their place in the quarter finals with a surprise win over Italy at Roker Park. Italy dominated the first half but could not make a breakthrough with Sandro Mazzola and Luigi Meroni flashing efforts just wide and Tarcisio Burgnich forcing goalkeeper Lev Yashin into a smart save.

The Soviet Union took the lead against the run of play when Igor Chislenko powered home a brilliant effort from the edge of the area in the 57th minute.

With full time creeping closer, Italy desperately pushed forward. Their best chance for an equalizer fell to Ezio Pascutti who could only fire a free header straight at Yashin.

ARGENTINA 0 WEST GERMANY 0

Argentina and West Germany played out a bad-tempered but entertaining goalless draw at Villa Park. The Argentine woodwork was rattled on two occasions during the first half as defender Roberto Perfumo twice looped a header over his goalkeeper only to be saved by the crossbar!

Germany's best opportunity of the match fell to Uwe Seeler who flashed an effort from inside the area just wide; while Argentina came close when Erminio Onega's driven free kick forced Hans Tilkowski into a spectacular diving save.

The most notable incident of the game occurred 25 minutes from time when Argentina's Rafael Albrecht was given his marching orders for a terribly mistimed challenge on Wolfgang Weber, which sparked an impassioned scuffle between the two sets of players.

ELSEWHERE...

GERMANO APPEARED FOR THE FIRST TIME FOR PORTUGAL AT OLD TRAFFORD, SCARING EVERYONE. EVEN HIS OWN TEAM MATES.

CONSEQUENTLY A BULGARIAN HEADED THE BALL INTO HIS OWN NET, SPECTACULARLY.

I'M A VERY UNHAPPY LOSER, SO LOOK OUT...

THAT'S EXACTLY WHAT I WANTED YOU TO DO. NOW WE CAN BE FRIENDS.

WHEN EUSEBIO, HIS HEAD STILL HELD TOGETHER WITH STICKING PLASTER, SHOT THE SECOND BULGARIA WERE FINISHED.

SHAME FOR APARUHOV, WHO IS THEIR ONE WORLD CLASS PLAYER, BUT GERMANO SAW TO HIM.

HOW MUCH MORE INJURY TIME, REF?

CHISLENKO SCORED A GREAT WINNER FOR RUSSIA AGAINST ITALY AT ROKER PARK, BREEZING PAST FACCHETTI BEFORE ALMOST BREAKING THE NET WITH HIS SHOT

IT MAY HAVE HURT FACCHETTI'S PRIDE, BUT IT SHOULDN'T AFFECT ITALY'S PROGRESS. THEY ONLY NEED TO BEAT THE NORTH KOREANS ON TUESDAY TO QUALIFY.

I HOPE THAT WASN'T TOO FAST FOR THE CAMERAMAN...

ARGENTINA 0 WEST GERMANY 0 LITTLE MORE TO BE SAID ABOUT THIS ONE.

THAT WAS THE SCORE AT HALF-TIME, TOO.

ARGENTINA'S ALBRECHT WAS SENT OFF FOR A MURDEROUS TACKLE ON WEBER, WHICH I'M NOT ALLOWED TO SHOW. IT WAS X-CERTIFICATE STUFF.

CENSORED

BY BOB HARRIS
author, broadcaster, former chief
correspondent for Thompson Regional
Newspapers and executive sports editor
of the Sunday Mirror

Brazil arrived in the North West of England in 1966 as undisputed world champions of the beautiful game and boasting the most accomplished and gifted player, the incomparable Pele, while looking for a hat-trick of triumphs to make the glittering Jules Rimet trophy their own.

They left after one victory in three games, defeated, disappointed and thoroughly bedraggled with Pele kicked and brutalised out of the competition.

Conspiracy theories abounded, mainly coming out of South America, that the tournament had been rigged in favour of the Europeans with questionable refereeing decisions punishing the likes of Brazil and Argentina, who also went out of the competition when their

competition was deemed by most as the dirtiest World Cup in history and the English fans were denied the opportunity of seeing the mercurial Pele at his best as the players of Bulgaria and Portugal kicked him out of the game without serious censure.

Son of a professional footballer and christened Edson Arantes do Nascimento, after the inventor Thomas Edison, the world knew him simply as Pele, while he also wore the nicknames Perola Negra (Black Pearl) and, more grandly, O Rei do Futebol (The King of Football). Strangely, his family always knew him as Dico!

By the time the World Cup arrived in England, Pele had already played in two winning World Cups, as a teenager in Sweden and then in Chile where injury again forced him onto the sidelines.

Two footed and a brilliant header of the ball despite standing only 5ft 8ins he beguiled all who watched him and in a 1281 game career (a figure disputed by some)

BUTCHERING DISGRACE TO

captain Rattin was sent off against England for violence of the tongue.

No one was more vociferous than former FIFA President Joao Havelange, a Brazilian, who asked: "Who was the FIFA President? Sir Stanley Rous, an Englishman. Where was the cup played? In England!

"In our three games against Portugal, Hungary and Bulgaria there were three referees and six assistants. Seven were English and two were German.

"Why do you think that happened? To destroy my team. And they destroyed it. Pele left injured."

The since discredited Brazilian, of course, talked arrant nonsense but it was almost backed up by fact as the

he is reputed to have scored exactly a goal a game for his home club Santos, Brazil and, finally, for New York Cosmos as American soccer struggled to find its feet.

The English public eagerly awaited his arrival and rubbed their hands in glee when he struck a trademark free kick, after being brought down, in the two goal win against Bulgaria, making him the first player to score in three World Cups.

The rugged Bulgarian team set about him to bring him down to their level and, sadly, there was little or no protection from the German referee Kurt Tschenscher and his linesmen who cautioned just two of the violent Bulgarians, Dobromir Jechev and Ivan Kolev, while the others seemed to take it in turns to bring down their tormentor. Brazil persevered 2-0.

But Pele was successfully kicked out of the next game against Hungary which the changed Brazilians lost 3-1 at Goodison Park in front of 51,387 fans, Brazil's first defeat in the competition since losing 4-2 to the same team in 1954.

Bruised, battered and patched up, Pele returned for the critical game against Portugal where all of us neutrals salivated at the thought of seeing the youthful talent of the outstanding Eusebio compared to the established qualities of Pele.

Portugal, who were to go on and challenge England in the semi finals, had taken careful note of just how the Bulgars had coped with Pele and they followed the example almost to the letter.

Brazil, with a confused selection policy after defeat and injuries, made seven changes with veterans Gilmar, Bellini, Djalma Santos and Garrincha all being axed and

runaway truck, leaving his team with ten men in the days before substitutions. Such is modern technology that the treatment of the world's greatest player can clearly be seen on YouTube in all its gory details.

It was only when Pele himself watched the flickering black and white reels of the game later that he realised just how badly he had been brutalised and he swore there and then that this would be his last World Cup.

Brazil flickered briefly when young left back Rildo embarked on a run which led to him scoring an excellent solo goal to bring the score to 2-1 but any further hopes were dashed when the star of the game, Eusebio, scored his second.

Pele rarely retaliated to his savage punishment by the hatchet men of the game. After being sent off early in his career he refused to retaliate again no matter how severe his treatment; he preferred to humiliate his opponents with his dazzling skills.

OF PELE WAS THE GAME

even before the injuries to Pele and Silva, Portugal looked the better team.

Pele was kicked, pushed, stamped on and generally abused to the chagrin of the 62,203 paying customers at Goodison Park who watched in amazement as lenient English referee George McCabe allowed it all to happen without taking action. Even in those tolerant times it was way beyond the limits.

Pele suffered most at the hands of his marker, the talented Benfica midfield star Mario Coluna, but it was two successive tackles from the diminutive Joao Morais which shocked the world of football – but left referee McCabe unmoved and the 25 year old was left to limp off looking like an old man who had been hit by a

Thankfully he was persuaded to renege on his threat to snub future World Cups and came back to play in the 1970 competition in Mexico where he, at last, displayed the full range of his many talents on the biggest stage as he helped his country and himself to a third Jules Rimet trophy victory with a 4-1 triumph over Italy in the final.

And for those fans in England left with the sour taste of his treatment on Merseyside there was the ever-lasting memory of his flashing header, brilliantly saved by Gordon Banks and, at the end of the 1-0 victory to the South Americans in 1970, his absolute respect for England captain Bobby Moore.

For those of my age Pele still rates ahead of modern greats like Messi and Ronaldo as the best player EVER!

BRAZIL 1 PORTUGAL 3

Rildo 72

Simoes 15
Eusebio 27, 85

BY SAM ELLIOTT

EUSEBIO eclipsed Pele as Portugal progressed to the quarter-finals on a day of high drama. Benfica star Eusebio stole the show at Goodison with two goals in the 3-1 defeat of Brazil but the match left a sour taste as Pele, unprotected by referee George McCabe, was given the hatchet treatment as had happened previously in the games with Bulgaria and Hungary. Pele, his right knee bandaged after a series of heavy tackles, left the game wrapped in a raincoat after limping around on the wing.

Eusebio had no part in that and deserved the praise that came his way for his two goals, one a header after 27 minutes and the second five minutes from the end.

Antonio Simoes headed Portugal in front after 15 minutes after Brazilian goalkeeper Manga had flapped at a cross. Eusebio doubled the lead 12 minutes later before Rildo gave double World Cup winners Brazil hope on 73 minutes with a low strike from outside the box which sped into the bottom corner. But Eusebio ended all argument with a rocket from the right side of the area.

THINK TWICE—THERE'LL BE
ANOTHER WORLD CUP IN FOUR YEARS ...

ARGENTINA 2 SWITZERLAND 0

Artime 53
Onega 81

BY SAM ELLIOTT

Luis Artime's skilful finish put Argentina in front eight minutes after half-time, having dominated the first period without scoring. The victory was confirmed in the 81st minute when Ermindo Onega, the River Plate attacking midfielder, latched onto a long ball, beat goalkeeper Leo Eichmann to the loose ball and ensured the Swiss would finish bottom.

MEXICO 0 URUGUAY 0

No such spectacle at Wembley for over 60,000 – Mexico could not find the goal they needed to beat Uruguay to take second place in the group. So Uruguay advanced to the final eight, where they knew they would have to produce more to have any hope of toppling much-fancied West Germany at Hillsborough.

Argentina went through, their 2-0 victory over Switzerland ends their group stage campaign with a second win, following on from the point well-earned by holding the Germans in the previous match.

LITTLE BIG MEN WHO

BY JOHN KEITH
author, broadcaster, stage presenter
and former northern football correspondent
of the Daily Express

They could have come from another planet. In football terms they did! But the North Korean adventure in the 1966 World Cup illuminated the tournament, their voyage ended by the galactic talents of Eusebio accompanied by a bizarre accusation from that luminary of Spaceship Football, Bill Shankly.

The little men from the most secretive nation on earth captivated spectators at England's greatest football festival and the watching public and pundits were plunged into a night of fantasy at Middlesbrough's old Ayresome Park home on the night of July 19, 1966.

It was football's equivalent of the peasants confronting the aristocracy…North Korea facing then two-times world champions Italy in Group 4.

The fact that the unknown warriors from the mysterious land on the north side of the 38th parallel – the dividing line in the aftermath of the 1950-53 Korean War – were in the tournament at all was down to football politics and a FIFA decision that angered a host of nations.

The world body allowed only one qualifying nation from Africa, Asia and Oceania combined, resulting in 20 countries withdrawing, leaving only North Korea and Australia to play off for a passage to the finals.

Two meetings in the neutral Cambodian capital of Phnom Penh ended in a 9-2 aggregate win for coach Myung Rye-Hun's Koreans, average height 5ft 5ins. But another problem lay in their path, threatening their trip to England.

After the Korean War, Britain refused to recognise the communist North and the Foreign Office were reluctant about granting the team visas to enter the UK.

It needed sensitive diplomacy from FIFA – how they could do with some of that today! – to persuade the British authorities to open the doors to the Koreans for an adventure still fondly recalled today on Teesside and Merseyside.

The team were nicknamed in their own land 'Chollima', a mythical winged horse symbolising North Korea's revolutionary spirit. But after checking into the St George Hotel at Teesside Airport they trained in front of many enthralled locals on the distinctly un-mythical stage of the ICI chemical works ground.

The spectators were impressed by the Korean speed and eager attacking style which would become their eye-catching trademarks during the finals.

Those qualities were not enough to trouble the Soviet Union, who beat the Koreans 3-0 in the opening group game, but when the Asian unknowns returned to Ayresome Park for their second game they held Chile to a 1-1 draw.

Italy needed only a draw to reach the quarter finals when they met the Koreans in their final group game. What ensued, though, was the stuff of legend.

With half an hour gone, Italy captain Giacomo Bulgarelli aggravated a knee problem in a challenge on Pak Seung-Zin, reducing his side to ten men for two thirds of the game in that pre-substitute era.

Shortly before the interval North Korea took full advantage when they headed an attempted Italian clearance back upfield. Pak Doo-Ik swept on to the ball before firing low past goalkeeper Enrico Albertosi.

There were subsequent missed chances at both ends but that goal ensured a sensational result, one that had sportswriters justifiably searching for the superlatives.

My former *Daily Express* colleague Arnold Howe wrote that "Pak Doo-Ik detonated one of the great explosions in soccer, that sent the non-entities of North Korea into the quarter finals and the Land of the Morning Calm

CHARMED WORLD

into a Middlesbrough night of frenzy."

As the exotic visitors headed down to Merseyside for an unforgettable quarter final collision with Portugal the Italian disgrace at their elimination manifested itself when Edmundo Fabbri's squad had a homecoming to forget, greeted with a hail of tomatoes and eggs when they arrived back at Genoa airport.

But the Italian legacy proved a curiously frightening one for their Asian conquerors. The Italians, convinced they would join the Soviets in qualifying from their group, had booked pre-quarter final accommodation on Merseyside at the Roman Catholic Loyola Hall, a Jesuit spirituality centre at Rainhill.

There was one massive problem…the venue spooked the atheist North Koreans, who were frightened by the religious statues and prevalence of crucifixes. Neither were they used to having single rooms and many insisted on sharing. One player screamed when he looked out of his window at night and saw an illuminated statue of Jesus.

It meant nights of fitful and fearful sleep for the visitors who, nevertheless, carried out their promise to the departed Italians to present a chalice to the hall which their group victims had planned in advance.

When the Koreans ran onto the Goodison Park pitch to face Portugal on Saturday afternoon, July 23, as the first Asian side to reach the World Cup last eight, we didn't quite know what to expect.

Portugal, parading great players like Mario Coluna, Alexandre Baptista and Antonio Simoes in addition to their star turn Eusebio, swept through their north west group with wins over Hungary, Bulgaria and Brazil.

Their 3-1 win over the Brazilians was marred by some crude challenges on Pele, forced to limp off the Goodison stage with a raincoat round his shoulders as a sad farewell to the only English club ground he played on.

But the way the Koreans had captured the public imagination with their exploits at Middlesbrough injected a fascinating ingredient into their collision with Portugal and almost instantly they were at it again, Pak Seung Zin scoring left footed from the edge of the box with one minute on the clock.

They made it 2-0 through Li Dong-Woon and the scoreline became unbelievable when Yang Seung-Kook made it 3-0 after 25 minutes. Football logic was being turned on its head. Cue Mozambique-born Eusebio da Silva Ferreira, the Black Panther, to restore sanity to the proceedings.

He latched onto a Simoes pass and fired right-footed past Korean keeper Chang-Myung and before the break Eusebio struck again from the penalty spot after a trip on Jose Torres.

With Korean energy levels visibly wilting, Eusebio completed Portugal's comeback from 0-3 to level by adding a powerful finish to a one-two with Simoes and before the hour mark the great man made it 4-3 after being fouled and despatching his second penalty – and fourth goal – of the match.

Jose Augusto nodded in Portugal's fifth after Torres headed back a Eusebio corner to round off an unforgettable match and one of the greatest individual displays. Eusebio's quartet of goals made Portugal only the second nation in World Cup history, after Austria in 1954, to win from a 3-0 deficit.

The Koreans were warmly saluted by the 40,248 Goodison crowd and taken to the hearts of the Merseyside public just as they had been on Teesside where, in the garden of a housing estate where Ayresome Park once stood, the bronze cast imprint of a football boot was laid on the spot Pak Doo-Ik unleashed his shot that toppled the Italians.

But at Goodison, that often outrageous but always

CONTINUED >>

charismatic Liverpool manager Bill Shankly, fresh from patrolling Goodison's dressing room corridor and tunnel, had a startling charge to make.

"They (the Koreans) cheated," Shankly claimed. "They changed half the team at half time because to most people they all look alike. But I could see they'd switched a few. Mind you, it didn't do them any good. Eusebio battered them."

The memories the Koreans left behind, though, are enduring and eight of their squad were enthusiastically welcomed in Liverpool and Middlesbrough when they made a return trip to England 36 years later in 2002, visiting Goodison and the site of former Ayresome Park.

Eusebio, too, returned to Goodison with his club Benfica in 2009, five years before his death. As he surveyed the stadium, doubtless recalling his master class decades earlier, his struggling English added a fitting charm to his comment when he said: "I like Goodness Park."

The misnomer was wonderful because that afternoon of July 26, 1966 he produced a display brimming with football goodness to end an Asian fairytale.

JULY 19TH – AYRESOME PARK 17,829
NORTH KOREA 1 ITALY 0

Pak Doo-Ik 41

BY JACK ROBERTS

The Italians missed two early chances by inches. The first attempt from Marino Perani was clawed over the bar by North Korean keeper Lee Chang-Myung, the second sent wide of the post by Perani.

The North Koreans weren't just there to defend. Midfielder Han Bong-Zin received an excellent chipped pass and dribbled himself into space but put the ball wide.

Then, half an hour into the game, the Italians were dealt a blow that may well have been fatal that day.

Midfielder Giacomo Bulgarelli made a sliding tackle on Pak Seung-Zin. The collision aggravated a knee injury and forced the Bologna player from the field. No substitutes were allowed.

Twelve minutes later came an even worse shock for the Azzurri.

A North Korean long ball from the halfway line was thumped back downfield by an Italian defender, but only as far as an onrushing North Korean defender, who delivered a thunderous headed ball that took one high bound into the path of 24-year-old Pak Doo-Ik who slotted the ball past Enrico Albertosi.

The ten-man Italians desperately surged forward to get an equalizer in the second half. The chances were there, but not one converted.

NORTH KOREA'S SHOCK DEFEAT OF ITALY MEANT AN EARLY RETURN HOME FOR ONE OF EUROPE'S MOST FANCIED TEAMS...

IN ROME, NAPLES AND MILAN, FANS WATCHED THE HORROR SHOW ON TELEVISION...

DIABOLICAL!

I'M JUST THINKING OF THE RECEPTION WE'LL GET WHEN WE STEP OFF THE PLANE...

IT WON'T BE A TRIUMPHANT ONE, THAT'S FOR SURE...

INSTEAD OF LANDING IN MILAN, AS EXPECTED, WHAT IF THE PLANE WAS TO SET DOWN ELSEWHERE?

ANYWHERE BUT MILAN, PILOT...

GENOA?

THAT WILL BE FINE...

A CLEVER IDEA, BUT IN GENOA...

THE WORD IS THAT THE ITALIAN TEAM IS ARRIVING **HERE** LATER TODAY

ROTTEN EGGS SPRING TO MIND...

...AND TOMATOES...

ON THE PLANE...

AT THE VERY LEAST WE'LL GET BACK HOME UNSEEN...

NOT QUITE...THERE WERE ENOUGH ANGRY FANS AT THE AIRPORT IN GENOA TO GIVE THE PLAYERS THE HOT RECEPTION THEY DESERVED...

MUCH ROTTEN FOODSTUFF WAS AIMED AT THE SHAME-FACED ITALIANS,

BRAZIL WERE ALSO ON THE WAY HOME.

PELE BOWS OUT

SO, TWO OF THE FAVOURITES TO WIN THE WORLD CUP HAD FAILED TO QUALIFY...

ENGLAND 2 FRANCE 0

Hunt 38, 75

BY SAM ELLIOT

NGLAND convincingly progressed to the World Cup quarter finals, but at what cost. Jimmy Greaves, their leading scorers and rated as one of the finest strikers in world football, finished the game with a deep gash on his shin that required 14 stitches.

"Don't ask me how it happened," he said. "I was unaware of it until I saw the blood pouring out of my sock after the game. It was right where the skin is tight over the bone."

Greaves' tournament was over – and he was to play only three more times for England in the next season.

As Greaves headed unknowingly to his greatest sporting heartbreak, up stepped Liverpool's Roger Hunt, the unselfish, magnificent workhorse who was always to be one of the first names penned in by Ramsey on his teamsheets.

Hunt scored both the goals that beat the French to send England forward to the quarter finals where Argentina waited.

England's victory came courtesy of a second half performance of real domination and character following a first 45 minutes of frustration which had drawn slow hand claps from the crowd.

All that changed with 38 minutes on the clock. A cross from Nobby Stiles was headed against the post by Jack Charlton and the rebound found Hunt in the right place to slot home as the French protested furiously for offside.

England had a Bobby Charlton effort ruled out after half-time before a cross from Ian Callaghan was nodded in by Hunt.

WEST GERMANY 2 SPAIN 1

Emmerich 39
Seeler 84

Fuste 23

West Germany finished top of Group 2 after coming from behind to condemn Jose Villalonga to defeat in his final game in charge of Spain. Spain needed a victory to avoid elimination and they took the lead midway through the first half as Jose Maria Fuste controlled a loose ball in the box and placed his shot into the bottom left hand corner.

West Germany levelled shortly before half time. A quickly-taken throw-in by Sigi Held caught the Spanish defence napping which allowed Lothar Emmerich to fire home his first goal of the tournament from a tight angle.

West Germany piled on the pressure and the winner arrived six minutes from time as Held's driven cross was emphatically finished by Seeler.

HUNGARY 3 BULGARIA 1

Davidov 43 (og)
Meszoly 45
Bene 54

Asparuhov 15

Hungary secured their place in the quarter finals with a hard-fought victory at Old Trafford. Bulgaria took the lead after 15 minutes as Georgi Asparukhov rounded the keeper before slotting home his country's first and only goal of the tournament.

The Bulgarians almost doubled their advantage as Dimitar Yakimov's goal-bound effort was desperately clawed away by Jozsef Gelei.

With 43 minutes on the clock Hungary drew level in fortunate circumstances. Bulgaria's Ivan Davidov powered a clearance into a teammate and the ball ricochet back into the net.

Hungary took the lead a minute later as Kalman Meszoly fired a half volley into the top corner. Ten minutes into the second half Bene headed home Imre Mathesz's low corner.

SOVIET UNION 2 CHILE 1

Porkujan 28, 85

Marcos 32

An under-strength Soviet Union maintained their 100 per cent record to put Chile out of the tournament in a free-flowing game. The Soviets took the lead just before the half hour as Valeriy Porkujan rifled a half volley into the roof of the net for his first international goal.

Chile came back with an almost immediate equaliser. Soviet keeper Anzor Kavazashvili spilled Leonel Sanchez's free kick and, from the resulting scramble, Ruben Marcos inadvertently deflected Guillermo Yavar's effort home to level the scores at the break.

The Soviet Union's winner arrived with just five minutes left on the clock as Porkujan latched onto a long punt forward before exquisitely lobbing the ball over Juan Olivares.

ENGLAND 1 ARGENTINA 0

Hurst 77

BY STUART HAMMONDS

Alf Ramsey likened them to animals, but the England manager was not talking about his group of Lions who progressed through the first knockout stage by grinding their way through an explosive encounter. Geoff Hurst's glancing header with 13 minutes left had the 90,000 Wembley crowd roaring with delight and Ramsey, the 46-year-old former defender, understandably took great pride in his side's solidity stretching to a fourth successive clean sheet.

But that doesn't tell half the story as the tournament hosts, dubbed the wingless wonders with a midfield four boosted by the energy of Blackpool youngster Alan Ball and West Ham's Martin Peters, but lacking real width, overcame a physical Argentinian side who played 55 minutes a man down.

Their captain, Antonio Rattin, was sent off with 35 minutes on the clock but took a further ten to leave the pitch, wiping his dirty hands on a corner flag bearing a Union Jack as he did.

The Great General, through which everything flowed in the South Americans' slow, cultured game, had not committed the latest foul on Hurst.

Racing Club defender Roberto Perfumo had clattered the forward from behind as he received a crisp pass from Bobby Moore, his Upton Park team-mate and captain for club and country, on the edge of the Argentine penalty area.

But Rattin took exception to referee Rudolf Kreitlein taking the name of yet another of his team – although the actual number was never confirmed – and pushed his protests too far.

Already booked himself, Rattin became the first man to be sent off at Wembley, apparently for abusing the West German official, who later said it was because he "did not like the look" in the eyes of the big midfielder.

"It was a tough game," said Rattin, "but no-one had been complaining about the tackles. The sending off should never have happened and it wouldn't have done if I could speak a word of German. All I wanted to do was talk to the referee, but the next thing I knew he was pointing off the pitch.

"Quiero a un interprete (I want an interpreter). I must have said it 20 or 30 times, pointing to my armband, but he couldn't understand a word I said. My voice is loud by nature and I am a big guy, but I was sent off simply for a misunderstanding. If I became heated, it was only after he had sent me off."

All hell broke loose as the Argentinian players surrounded Kreitlein, who needed back-up from several FIFA officials and police before the game could restart.

It eventually did, in an even more cynical atmosphere than before. Petty fouling was the norm, but Ramsey's men eventually found a way around the persistent body checks.

Hurst, the 24-year-old in for the injured Jimmy Greaves, had gone close on two occasions early on. Latching on to a huge kick from goalkeeper Gordon Banks, he stretched the Argentinian defence two minutes in, with Bobby Charlton's resulting corner striking the outside of the post.

Moments later, Nobby Stiles intercepted a loose pass from Rattin and the Manchester United midfielder, Liverpool striker Roger Hunt and Charlton combined to set up Hurst for a left-foot shot that was turned behind by keeper Antonio Roma.

Roma denied the Hammers hitman again early in the second half, but just as it looked as if the ten men might keep England out, Hurst expertly met an inviting cross from Peters to book a semi-final spot.

Alf Ramsey steps in to stop England's George Cohen swapping his shirt with the Argentines

Everton left-back Ray Wilson fed Peters – described by Ramsey as being "ten years ahead of his time" – who delivered an outswinger with his left boot for Hurst, angling his run across the near post six yards out, to head the ball into the far corner of the net with the faintest of touches.

Ball and Charlton both went close to putting the result beyond doubt, something no-one was left with when wondering what Ramsey thought of the visitors' behaviour.

The ex-Ipswich Town boss took matters into his own hands when the Argentinians tried to swap shirts with his players at the end of the game, George Cohen's jersey stretched beyond recognition as Ramsey pulled it back from a South American opponent.

"Alf saw what was happening and he rushed over, saying 'You're not changing shirts with him' – or words to that effect," said Cohen. "He was incensed by the way they played. Tackling is fine, but it was some of the snidey things; the spitting and pulling the short hairs on your neck, pulling your ear."

The chaos continued into the tunnel, where Argentinian players reportedly urinated against the wall after threatening ref Kreitlein, who needed police protection, and officials.

"It seemed a pity so much Argentinian talent is wasted," blasted an indignant Ramsey. "Our best football will come against the right type of opposition – a team who come to play football, and not act as animals."

Into the last four, the Three Lions would get the opportunity to back up their manager's words. Portugal and the brilliant Eusebio lay in wait.

WEST GERMANY 4 URUGUAY 0

Haller 11, 83
Beckenbauer 70
Seeler 75

BY HUGO VARLEY

West Germany eased into the semi-finals with an emphatic victory over nine-man Uruguay at Hillsborough. It was the South Americans who started the game as the brighter side and they came inches away from taking the lead when Julio Cortes' free kick cannoned off the bar.

Uruguay's Pedro Rocha then had a header controversially cleared off the line by Karl-Heinz Schnellinger, with the replay suggesting that the German defender may have used his hand to block the ball.

With eleven minutes on the clock West Germany took the lead in rather fortunate circumstances.

Sigi Held weaved through a couple of challenges before scuffing a weak effort which appeared to be heading harmlessly into the arms of Ladislao Mazurkiewicz in the Uruguay goal. However his shot cannoned off Helmut Haller and wrong-footed Mazurkiewicz to send the Germans into the lead.

Just before half time West Germany came close to doubling their advantage with a Franz Beckenbauer free kick. The midfielder's driven effort from 30 yards produced a spectacular save from Mazurkiewicz.

The game was ultimately decided by a ten-minute period of madness from Uruguay at the start of the second half.

Three minutes after the break Uruguay's captain Horacio Troche was given his marching orders for an off-the-ball incident where he appeared to strike Lothar Emmerich; Troche was then quickly joined in the dressing room by Hector Silva who was sent off for kicking out at Haller.

The two dismissals tilted the balance into West Germany's favour and they went on to dominate the rest of the match.

Uruguay defended valiantly but a second goal appeared inevitable as Seeler and Beckenbauer crashed efforts against the woodwork.

With 20 minutes remaining Uruguay's resolve finally broke and the floodgates eventually opened as West Germany grabbed three goals in quick succession

First, Beckenbauer played a brilliant one-two with Seeler before calmly rounding the keeper and tapping the ball home; then Seeler put the game beyond doubt when he took advantage of a tired looking Uruguay defence to power home an effort from the right hand side of the box.

The scoring was rounded off seven minutes from time when Haller coolly slotted the ball home for his second after being presented with a glorious opportunity following a slip by Jorge Manicera.

PORTUGAL 5 NORTH KOREA 3

Eusebio 27, 43 (pen), 56, 59 (pen)
Jose Augusto 80

Pak Seung-Zin 1
Li Dong-Woon 22
Yang Seung-Kook 25

BY JACK ROBERTS

N orth Korea had shocked the world when they beat Italy and they weren't done! Within 25 minutes of kick-off in their quarter final date with Portugal, they had built a 3-0 lead and looked ready to continue their remarkable run. Then Eusebio intervened.

The Black Panther scored his first goal two minutes after North Korea's third and ended the day with four goals in leading his country to five unanswered scores and a 5-3 win.

Pak Seung-Zin put the Koreans ahead after just one minute and further first half goals came from Li Dong-Woon and Yang Seung-Kook.

But Eusebio struck in the 27th, 43rd (from a penalty), 56th and 59th minute (another penalty) to end the fairy tale. Jose Augusto wrapped it up ten minutes from time.

SOVIET UNION 2 HUNGARY 1

Chislenko 5
Porkujan 46

Bene 57

BY SAM JACKSON

H ungary were dominated from the kick off, perhaps intimidated by a country that had savagely repressed an uprising in Budapest only 10 years earlier. The Soviets took an early lead when Igor Chislenko pounced on a fumble by Hungarian goalkeeper Antal Szentmihalyi and they doubled it shortly after half time through Valery Porkujan.

Ference Bene got a goal back from a tight angle after 57 minutes, but despite further pressure the Magyars could do no more and were on their way home, as deflated as the match ball which burst after being booted onto the clock stand roof.

WEST GERMANY 2 SOVIET UNION 1

Haller 42
Beckenbauer 67

Porkujan 88

BY JOHN LYONS

WHILE England were gearing up for their semi-final against Eusebio's Portugal, West Germany and the Soviet Union had the chance to be the first team into the final. An expectant crowd of 38,273 packed into Goodison Park for the showdown and ultimately it was a moment of magic from young midfielder Franz Beckenbauer that made the difference.

In a physical encounter, the Soviet Union's legendary goalkeeper Lev Yashin, 36, was a steadying presence for his side early on. However, he wasn't able to stop the Germans landing the first blow three minutes before the break.

West Germany defender Karl-Heinz Schnellinger was allowed to advance into Soviet territory without anyone closing him down. With time and space to work with, the 27-year-old produced a superb ball to release Helmut Haller.

There was still plenty for the midfielder to do, but in an instant, from the right-hand side of the penalty area, he flashed a shot past Yashin and into the corner of the net. It was his fifth goal of a fruitful tournament.

If that was a blow for the Soviet Union so close to half-time, there was worse to follow. Just a minute later Igor Chislenko was sent off to leave his side a goal and a man down.

A hobbling Chislenko lost the ball to Germany's Siegfried Held and, in pure frustration, kicked out at his opponent. Italian referee Concetto Lo Bello had little hesitation in sending him for an early bath.

With the clock advancing in the second half and still only one goal in it, West Germany needed a second to make the game safe.

Cometh the hour, cometh the man. Bayern Munich midfielder Beckenbauer, only 20, decided to take matters into his own hands. He beat one man, ran on and then cracked a 25-yard screamer high into the net. A startled Yashin was caught flat-footed and the game appeared to be up.

But credit to the Soviet Union, they fought to the end despite being a man down. West Germany goalkeeper Hans Tilkowski had earlier suffered a blow to his shoulder and perhaps it was playing on his mind late on.

When a ball was crossed into the box, the 31-year-old lost it under pressure and the Soviet Union's Valeriy Porkujan had the simple task of knocking the loose ball into the empty net from close in.

There were just two minutes left on the clock, though, and West Germany held on in a nervy finish. But who would they meet in the final? They were about to find out...

ENGLAND 2 PORTUGAL 1

B Charlton 30, 80

Eusebio 82 (pen)

BY JACK ROBERTS

England manager Alf Ramsey had found himself under fierce pressure from FIFA and even his own FA to drop Nobby Stiles from his World Cup team. The gap-toothed Manchester United terrier had caught Jacques Simon with a bad tackle in the match against France. But Ramsey stuck defiantly by his man, defending him as hard but fair.

Stiles had gone on to prove his worth in the battle with Argentina; now in the semi-final with Portugal he was to be England's star, man-marking the lethal Eusebio out of the game.

Stiles, who played every minute of England's campaign, was so effective that Eusebio became a forlorn figure.

Away from the heat of that two-man battle, this thrilling semi-final was marked by its fine sportsmanship.

Many of the 94,000 Wembley crowd had arrived in trepidation at the thought of the dazzling Portuguese attacking threat of Eusebio, Simoes, Augusto and Torres.

But the England defence, with Stiles to the fore, proved superior.

Bobby Charlton, showing his world class in the central midfield role Ramsey had persuaded him to undertake from his more familiar left wing position, scored both England's goals.

In the 30th minute, with England counter-attacking, he scored his first. Ray Wilson stabbed the ball through to where Roger Hunt fashioned a shot. Goalkeeper Jose Pereira, who had shown a little shakiness in earlier attacks, decided to deal with this one by sliding feet first at it. The ball came back to Charlton who smashed it home from 18 yards.

The support England were given by the crowd echoed and re-echoed around the stadium, and Wembley exploded in raptures of delight after 80 minutes as they scored their second. Martin Peters, again showing his fine touches, had a shot charged down. He retrieved the ball and quickly fed it back to Charlton who again unleashed a rocket, this time from 15 yards into the back of the net.

Portugal were by no means finished, and, two minutes later, Jack Charlton, in a despairing attempt to stop a header from Torres entering the net, pushed the ball out with his hand. Eusebio, in his one decisive act of the game, scored his eighth goal of the tournament with the penalty. It was the first goal conceded by England in the tournament.

Bobby Charlton unleashes his shot for the opening goal

PORTUGAL 2 SOVIET UNION 1

Eusebio 12 (pen)
Torres 89

Malofeyev 43

BY HUGO VARLEY

Portugal bounced back from the disappointment of losing to England in the semi-finals by securing third place in dramatic circumstances at Wembley. With the game seemingly destined for extra time Jose Torres powered a volley past Lev Yashin with one minute remaining to end Portugal's World Cup journey on a high.

The match began at a fast tempo and Portugal quickly broke the deadlock from the penalty spot with 12 minutes on the clock.

The referee was given no option but to award a spot kick after Murtaz Khurtsilava had blatantly handled the ball when trying to clear Festa's looping free kick.

Eusebio firmly placed the penalty out of reach of the diving Yashin to net his ninth goal of the tournament.

Despite this early setback the Soviet Union grew into the first half and came close to levelling the score through Slava Metreveli. The speedy winger brilliantly weaved through a couple of challenges before having an effort well saved by Jose Pereira in the Portugal goal.

Two minutes before half time the Soviet Union scrambled home a deserved equaliser.

After an impressive passing move the ball found its way to Metreveli on the right hand side of the box. The 30-year-old's driven effort was then spilled by Pereira, which allowed Eduard Malofeyev to bundle the ball into the net and level the scores at the break.

It was certainly a scrappy equaliser and although the goal was awarded to Malofeyev most Soviet players initially ran to celebrate with his strike partner Anatoli Banishevski, believing at first that he had got the final touch.

In the second half the Soviet Union continued efficiently to restrict the dangerous Eusebio and they came close to taking the lead on 65 minutes when the hugely impressive Metreveli fired a rasping effort just wide.

Shortly after this Nikolai Morozov's side thought they had won a penalty. Malofeyev did brilliantly to get on the end of a loose ball and appeared to be bundled over in the box by Pereira; however much to the despair of the Soviet players the 24-year-old was flagged offside by the linesman.

Despite being restricted by the Soviet defence, Portugal did show glimpses of attacking flare during the second half and they ultimately snatched victory right at the death.

Torres did brilliantly to shake off his marker and latch onto Jose Augusto's flick before rifling a volley into the top left hand corner from eight yards.

Otto Gloria's side could actually have made the score line more convincing in the final few seconds but Yashin did well to deny Augusto's ambitious effort from a tight angle.

ALF'S SECRET NIGHT VISIT TO A FLEET STREET PAL – WAS GREAVES ON HIS MIND?

PATRICK COLLINS
Seven times Sports Writer of the Year
Mail on Sunday

It was shortly after eight on a July evening when Alf Ramsey set out from the Hendon Hall hotel. Twenty minutes later, he stood on the doorstep of a suburban home in North London. The door was opened by a young boy and Alf, with customary cordiality, barked: "What are you doing up at this time of night? You ought to be in bed!" The lad was bewildered, until he heard his father's voice behind him in the hall. "It's all right, Niall," said Reg Drury. "It's Mr Ramsey."

Mr Ramsey, of course, was the manager of England, and three days later the team he had created would be contesting the final of the World Cup just a few miles down the road. Drury was the chief football writer of the *News of the World*, and he was preparing for the most important match of his long career. The two men had known each other for almost 20 years, from the days when Alf was playing right back for Tottenham and Reg was covering Spurs for the local paper. Each was easy in the other's company, and they sat and talked for a couple of hours until Alf glanced at his watch and announced that he must be getting back. The old friends shook hands. "All the best on Saturday, Alf," said Reg. "Thank you, Reg," replied Alf, and he set off on another stroll through the drowsy streets.

Now this seems an unremarkable tale, until we consider the context. In the course of England's World Cup campaign, Ramsey had become one of the most familiar figures in English life. Although he would have hated the notion, he was a "celebrity". As such, and especially at this critical time, his views were keenly sought and his company was coveted. And Drury worked for the largest-selling newspaper in the land, a paper that sold more than six million copies every Sunday. Of course, the final would be played before the *News of the World* was published, but the background tales, the untold stories, all these would have been invaluable to coverage in the wake of the match.

Yet Alf's secrets were safe with Reg. Drury respected Ramsey's trust, just as Alf had known he would.

A similar scenario would be quite impossible today. For one thing, a modern national manager could not afford a similar relationship with a member of the media. He may have his friends in the Press, but he has a hundred more pressing demands upon his time and energy. There is also that matter of "celebrity". In the age of 24 – hour rolling news, of camera phones and incessantly chattering social media, the notion that an England manager might stroll the streets of London, unchallenged and unheeded, just days before a World Cup Final at Wembley is quite unthinkable. But 1966 was another era, another world.

A year or so after that famous game, I became a colleague and in time a firm friend of Reg. I used to marvel at this fiercely conscientious reporter, and at the way he had acquired a vast amount of football contacts, people who would supply him with an apparently endless stream of well-researched and soundly based "exclusives". But I knew nothing of his meeting with Alf until some years after Ramsey had departed the England post in 1974. Reg was reminiscing about Alf's quirky ways and, in an unguarded moment, he spoke of the way in which Ramsey had greeted his son when young Niall opened the door one evening. "Alf?" I said. "Round your place? When was that? Reg was furious with himself. He supplied the barest details, and would not be drawn.

"But what about Jim?" I asked. "You must have made a case for Jim?" Now Reg idolised Jimmy Greaves. He saw in the little fellow all the virtues he most revered in a footballer. He understood Alf's motives in preferring Geoff Hurst, but I sensed that Reg would have played Greaves, regardless of consequence. "Come on," I urged. "You told him why he had to play Jim, didn't you?" He smiled a brief smile, knowing precisely how Ramsey would have reacted had anybody – especially a reporter – been bold enough to instruct him in matters of strategy or selection.

"The thing about Alf," said Reg, "was that he knew what he wanted, and he knew how to get it. He'd always been like that. I always thought he'd do well for himself." In truth, his old friend was an excellent judge. Alf Ramsey did very well for all of us.

Alf Ramsey with his England squad

Below: Reg Drury, right, at a Football Writers' Awards night with FWA chairman Dennis Signy, centre, and Gordon Banks

THE FINAL

BY STEVE CURRY
Chief Football Writer
Daily Express
Sports Reporter of the Year
Sunday Telegraph

Alf Ramsey had pondered long and hard, weighed the pros and cons, on the only real decision he had to make on the composition of his side to play in the final. Should it be the international rookie Geoff Hurst or the maverick Jimmy Greaves, a workhorse or a one-off genius, who played the game by instinct. Hurst had replaced the injured Greaves in the quarter-final against Argentina, scored and had an assist in one of the semi final goals against Portugal.

It has always been claimed Ramsey mistrusted players whose unpredictability could win a game but could not guarantee a high octane performance every time. To Alf, Greaves was a luxury player who fitted uneasily into his

He and Hurst were told they were playing the night before the game though Greaves was not told his fate until the morning of the game, perhaps, on reflection, a managerial mistake.

So it was that the dye was cast as the players waited for their moment of history at The Hendon Hall Hotel in North London. These, of course, were the days long before players earned mind-boggling sums of money. These were mere mortal footballers rather than the superstars of the modern generation. One of Ramsey's bonding favourites when the squads were together was a night at the cinema, invariably to see a Western, for which type of film Ramsey had a predilection. Over time this was the cause of much mirth with cries of "seen it already" quite common. But the manager usually prevailed, so Hendon cinema goers were shocked when 22 players and the England staff turned up at Hendon 'flicks so close to their day of destiny.

This time, though, no Western was being shown. Instead the England players watched *Those Magnificent*

MAGNIFICENT THE WINNING

system. In the end it was not to prove Greaves' day and for 50 years it has been a matter of regret to him and probably one of the triggers that catapulted the little virtuoso into finding solace in alcohol.

Bobby Moore, as Ramsey's captain, was one of the first to be told of his decision. He was Jimmy's roommate and had thought that, fit again, he would automatically regain his place. Others in the squad were less convinced, including the Charlton brothers. They saw Hurst as more suited to the side and its modus operandi, the ideal target man. Alf could, of course, have chosen to drop Roger Hunt but this did not enter the manager's head. The Liverpool man was Alf's kind of player, reliable, industrious, under-stated and had performed consistently in the pre-tournament tour of Scandinavia and Poland. Hunt would not be dropped.

Men in their Flying Machines; perhaps appropriate for what they were about to achieve.

The England of 2016 are isolated from the outside world throughout the period of a competition, invariably in a closely-guarded, security-ridden hotel. In 1966 things were hugely different with access to the players easy and open. Saturday morning shoppers in Hendon thus had the chance to wish the England players all the best for the match that day as they strolled around the High Street shops, getting there not by limousine with a minder but by hopping onto a London Transport bus. Time drags for players before a big game so they were delighted eventually to board their coach for the short journey to the home of football and the comforting sight

It's all over, Geoff Hurst makes it 4-2

wishes, the mood briefly lightened when one "blazer" muttered "all the best George" not realising he was addressing Ray Wilson and not George Cohen. The morning rain had abated by the time the players walked up the famous Wembley tunnel to be introduced to the Queen.

There was a tentative start to the game with German defenders backing off and allowing easy movements from midfield forward. Martin Peters and Alan Ball in wide positions were being orchestrated by Bobby Charlton, who was settling the team down with his apparent composure and that hallmark flowing movement.

An early chance. A Nobby Stiles cross was headed away by Horst Hottges but picked up by Charlton. In clearing the cross from Hurst's forehead Tilkowski knocked himself out, needing treatment. England had settled well. Jack Charlton entered the action setting

of Wembley's Twin Towers. Meanwhile, Helmut Schoen, manager of the the West German opposition had been checking on his own selection problems. Their young rising star, Franz Beckenbauer had to be cleared to play by FIFA's disciplinary committee over a caution that

MEN BECOME MACHINE

proved to be a case of mistaken identity. There was also a decision to be made about goalkeeper Hans Tilkowski who had taken several hits in the Goodison Park semi-final against the USSR. But the Borussia Dortmund keeper had been excellent in the group stages and Schoen felt the urge to retain him.

With Wembley packed long before the 3pm kick-off, the atmosphere was increasingly electrifying. The band of the Royal Marines played the music and rarely has the National Anthem been sung with greater fervour. In the Press gallery, slung under the roof high above the Royal Box, the sense of anticipation was heightening and, for this young sports reporter, the excitement produced a tingling I can still recapture 50 years on.

In the England dressing room there was pandemonium as FA counsellors and staff popped in to give their best

Peters free and Tilkowski was in action again, turning the shot round his post. The German were agitating the England players and their fans by some over reaction to tackles and Swiss referee Gottfried Dienst warned Cologne's Wolgang Weber for his histrionics.

Suddenly there was shocked silence from the terraces as Germany took a tenth minute lead as a result of a defensive error that was so untypical of what had been England's strongest asset – defence. From the left Sigi Held lofted a cross. Gordon Banks told Wilson to leave it believing it would pass wide but the Everton defender decided to head it and ball dropped at the feet of Helmut Haller who had time to compose and pivot before sending the ball to Banks' right.

It was time for re-grouping and within six minutes

CONTINUED >>

THE FINAL

England were level. Wolfgang Overath had been warned for a heavy challenge on Ball and now caught Bobby Moore's ankle. The skipper took the kick quickly arching his cross to the far post where Hurst was coming in to head down and past Tilkowski. Hurst was smothered and it was another timely reminder of the part West Ham players played in the World Cup success, the axis of Moore, Hurst and Peters.

It was now a riveting contest. Bobby Charlton was at the heart of the action, probing, switching play and testing Tilkowski himself with a shot saved only at the second attempt. England seemed in control. Moore, majestic, dominating, almost arrogantly brought the ball out of defence. But it was not all one way. The ebullient Ball was occasionally getting caught in possession. On one such occasion the long legs of Jack Charlton, like the tentacles of an octopus, came to England's rescue at the cost of a corner. The result was a shot from Overath, beaten out by Banks, but immediately Lothar Emmerich hammered in back for the keeper to save. It was now a fluctuating game and the the first half ended with Banks tipping an Overath shot over the bar.

England appealed for a penalty early in the second half when Bobby Charlton went down under a challenge from sweeper Willi Schulz but the claim was denied. However, England seemed to be increasingly in control, the flow of the play mainly in the direction of Tilkowski's goal. The game unceasingly appeared to be moving England's way and it seemed inevitable that a goal would come. Yet it took until the 78th minute. Hunt, whose contribution was tireless but who had been well policed, now made a key contribution. His pass to Ball

Bobby Charlton holds the trophy flanked by Alan Ball, left, and Bobby Moore

RESULTS

GROUP 1

ENGLAND	0-0	URUGUAY
FRANCE	1-1	MEXICO

Hausser 62 — Borja 48

URUGUAY	2-1	FRANCE

Rocha 26, Cortes 31 — De Bourgoing 15 (pen)

ENGLAND	2-0	MEXICO

B. Charlton 37, Hunt 75

MEXICO	0-0	URUGUAY
ENGLAND	2-0	FRANCE

Hunt 38, 75

	P	W	D	L	F	A	PTS
ENGLAND	3	2	1	0	4	0	5
URUGUAY	3	1	2	0	2	1	4
MEXICO	3	0	2	1	1	3	2
FRANCE	3	0	1	2	2	5	1

GROUP 2

WEST GERMANY	5-0	SWITZERLAND

Held 16, Haller 21, 77 (pen), Beckenbauer 40, 52

ARGENTINA	2-1	SPAIN

Artime 65, 77 — Pirri 67

SPAIN	2-1	SWITZERLAND

Sanchis 57, Amancio 75 — Quentin 31

ARGENTINA	0-0	WEST GERMANY
ARGENTINA	2-0	SWITZERLAND

Artime 52, Onega 79

WEST GERMANY	2-1	SPAIN

Emmerich 39, Seeler 84 — Fuste 23

	P	W	D	L	F	A	PTS
WEST GERMANY	3	2	1	0	7	1	5
ARGENTINA	3	2	1	0	4	1	5
SPAIN	3	1	0	2	4	5	2
SWITZERLAND	3	0	0	3	1	9	0

GROUP 3

BRAZIL	2-0	BULGARIA

Pele 15, Garrincha 63

PORTUGAL	3-1	HUNGARY

Jose Augusto 1, 67, Torres 90 — Bene 60

HUNGARY	3-1	BRAZIL

Bene 2, Farkas 64, Meszoly 73 (pen) — Tostao 14

PORTUGAL	3-0	BULGARIA

Vutsov 17 (o.g.), Eusebio 38, Torres 81

PORTUGAL	3-1	BRAZIL

Simoes 15, Eusebio 27, 85 — Rildo 70

HUNGARY	3-1	BULGARIA

Davidov 43 (o.g.), Meszoly 45, Bene 54 — Asparuhov 15

	P	W	D	L	F	A	PTS
PORTUGAL	3	3	0	0	9	2	6
HUNGARY	3	2	0	1	7	5	4
BRAZIL	3	1	0	2	4	6	2
BULGARIA	3	0	0	3	1	8	0

led to Tilkowski turning the resultant shot for a corner. Ball took it, the ball falling to Hurst. His shot was deflected by Schulz and Peters was there, unmarked to steer his half-volley into the net.

We believed it was game over, the eulogies were being composed in an animated Press gallery. The glory hour was at hand. But no. With seconds of the 90 minutes remaining, Jack Charlton was penalised, harshly, jumping to a header. Emmerich's free-kick seemed to hit Karl-Heinz Schnellinger on the arm but referee Deinst saw no offence and at the far post Weber drove in the equaliser. A draw.

Ramsey, famously, told his deflated players: "You've won it once, go and win it again." More importantly, he was telling them to look how the Germans had socks round their ankles. They were tired and England still had the upper hand. It was simple but effective psychology. One man was already overcoming his tiredness. Ball was ready to run and run, which he did for the extra 30 minutes. The extended time started well for England. Ball tried his luck from 20 yards, Tilkowski tipped over. The German keeper finger-tipped a Bobby Charlton effort against his upright. Germany were, indeed, tired. But when England's third goal came it was shrouded in controversy.

Ball, a bundle of energy, created another opening on the right, which he fed to Hurst. The striker manoeuvred to get in a rising shot on the turn which Tilkowski touched onto the underside of his crossbar. As the ball fell the nearest England player Hunt immediately called the ball over the line. The Germans claimed it had dropped on the line and Deinst went to consult his

Russian linesman Tofik Bakhramov who found his place in history by insisting the ball had indeed crossed the line.It is a controversy that is debated today.

Germany were now flattened. Heavy-legged and dispirited they had little left to offer though Held and Seeler battled bravely. The crowd were ecstatic, the mood pulsating as those seconds ticked away. But Moore had one more indelible mark to leave on the game. He took a pass from Ball, found Hurst and the West Ham telepathy took over. Though now shattered, Hurst took his team-mate's pass on his chest 12 yards inside the German half, turned, paused and then headed forward. Three fans were on the pitch thinking the game was over as the crowd whistled. Hurst ploughed on and with his last ounce of energy drove his shot into the roof of the net.

Jack Charlton sank to his knees, his brother cried. The whistle had gone. Game over. Reserves on their feet. Alf vindicated in his team selection. Hurst a hat-trick hero. There were tears in the Press gallery too, not least from this observer. The players forgot their exhaustion. They had made history that has still to be repeated. Many hours later in the foyer of the newly-built Royal Garden Hotel, I was giving Alan Ball a piggy-back. We were as one, players and critics.

Indeed the country celebrated, the feel-good factor spreading, fanning the fire of pride. There was one final gesture, which summed up the Summer of '66. Nobody had thought about money but Ramsey was informed that £22,000 was on offer to the players. At the captain's initiative, the money was split equally among the squad of 22. Now that is class.

GROUP 4

SOVIET UNION	**3-0**	**NORTH KOREA**
Malofeyev 31, 88		
Banishevskiy 33		
ITALY	**2-0**	**CHILE**
Mazzola 8		
Barison 88		
CHILE	**1-1**	**NORTH KOREA**
Marcos 26 (pen)		Pak Seung-zin 88
SOVIET UNION	**1-0**	**ITALY**
Chislenko 57		
NORTH KOREA	**1-0**	**ITALY**
Pak Doo-Ik 42		
SOVIET UNION	**2-1**	**CHILE**
Porkujan 28, 85		Marcos 32

	P	W	D	L	F	A	PTS
SOVIET UNION	3	3	0	0	6	1	6
NORTH KOREA	3	1	1	1	2	4	3
ITALY	3	1	0	2	2	2	2
CHILE	3	0	1	2	2	5	1

QUARTER FINALS

PORTUGAL	**5-3**	**NORTH KOREA**
Eusebio 27, 43 (pen),		Pak Seung-Zin 1
56, 59 (pen)		Li Dong-Woon 22
Jose Augusto 80		Yang Seung-Kook 25
WEST GERMANY	**4-0**	**URUGUAY**
Haller 11, 83		
Beckenbauer 70		
Seeler 75		
SOVIET UNION	**2-1**	**HUNGARY**
Chislenko 5		Bene 57
Porkujan 46		
ENGLAND		**1-0 ARGENTINA**
Hurst 78		

SEMI FINALS

WEST GERMANY	**2-1**	**SOVIET UNION**
Haller 42		Porkujan 88
Beckenbauer 67		
ENGLAND	**2-1**	**PORTUGAL**
B. Charlton 30, 80		Eusebio 82 (pen)

THIRD PLACE MATCH

PORTUGAL	**2-1**	**SOVIET UNION**
Eusebio 12 (pen)		Malofeyev 43
Torres 89		

FINAL

ENGLAND	**4-2** **(A.E.T.)**	**WEST GERMANY**
Hurst 18, 101, 120		Haller 12, Weber 89
Peters 78		

TEAM OF THE TOURNAMENT

Goalkeeper	Defenders	Midfielders	Forwards
Gordon Banks (Eng)	George Cohen (Eng)	Franz Beckenbauer (Ger)	Florian Albert (Hun)
	Bobby Moore (Eng)		Uwe Seeler (Ger)
	Vicente Lucas (Por)	Mario Coluna (Por)	Eusebio (Por)
	Silvio Marzolini (Arg)	Bobby Charlton (Eng)	

1966 AND ALL THAT!

The year of 1966 in sport may have been dominated by England's World Cup triumph. But there were other significant happenings...not least the rematch between Henry Cooper and the newly-dubbed Muhammad Ali.

Clay had beaten Cooper three years earlier in the fifth round at Wembley Stadium in a match marred by controversy after he had been decked by the famous Cooper left hook 'Enry's 'Ammer'.

A split in Clay's glove, made worse by trainer Angelo Dundee deliberately sticking his fingers inside, caused a delay and Clay came back in the next round to stop Cooper with a barrage of vicious punches which opened a deep, pumping gash in the Englishman's left eye.

Cooper was to suffer the same fate at Highbury on May 21, 1966 when the 24-year-old Ali, now world champion after beating Sonny Liston, stopped him in the sixth round in front of 40,000.

Cooper, aged 32, fought bravely with his big left hooks to battle against Ali's quick footwork and fast punches. But another blistering right hand opened up Cooper's left eye, which later required 12 stitches, and ended his world championship dream.

On the cricket front, England's fast bowling sensation John Snow turned master batsman with a last-wicket century stand at the Oval in the fifth Test against Gary Sobers' West Indies.

Snow and fellow paceman Ken Higgs put on 128 as England amassed a mighty 527 in the first innings. Snow scored 59 not out and Higgs 63.

Tom Graveney, with 165, and wicketkeeper John Murray, with 112, led a batting line up which included Geoff Boycott, John Edrich, Basil D'Oliveira and Brian Close.

England went on to win the match by an innings and 34 runs but lost the five-match series 3-1.

Sobers enjoyed spectacular success in the series, scoring 722 runs at an average of 103.14 with three centuries, and had 20 wickets at 27.25, as well as taking ten catches.

In domestic football, Fulham, bottom of the Division One table, with one victory since October, defeated title favourites Liverpool 2-0 on February 26. Steve Earle scored both goals, maestro Johnny Haynes pulled the strings and Liverpool's Ian St John was sent off two minutes from time for punching Mark Pearson. Liverpool did go on to win the title by six points from Leeds. Fulham finished 20th, just ahead of the relegated Northampton Town and Blackburn Rovers.

Particularly close to cartoonist Bob Bond's heart was Preston's 2-1 defeat of Spurs in the FA Cup fifth round. Preston, near the foot of Division Two, derailed the mighty Tottenham Cup bid with goals from Alex Dawson and Ernie Hannigan after Jimmy Greaves had given Spurs an early lead.

Sadly for Bob and Preston, they went out in the next round, beaten 3-1 in a replay by Manchester United.

United featured in one of the best European performances on the year on March 9, beating Benfica 5-1 at their Stadium of Light, inspired by a 19-year-old called George Best. As a preview to the World Cup, Nobby Stiles kept a firm rein on Eusebio.

United won the quarter final tie 8-3 on aggregate but went out in the semi-final 2-1 to Partizan Belgrade who lost the final 2-1 to Real Madrid.

COOPER V ALI AGAIN...

WELL 'ENRY, YOU'VE GIVEN US SOME GREAT MEMORIES DOWN THE YEARS...

BRIAN LONDON OUTBOXED TO WIN THE BRITISH AND COMMONWEALTH TITLES MANY MOONS AGO...

PICK RICHARDSON TRIED TO TAKE THEM FROM YOU.

JOHNNY PRESCOTT ALSO HAD A GO, BUT WAS BEATEN INTO SUBMISSION.

SO CASSIUS CLAY RETURNED, OR MUHAMMAD ALI, AS HE NOW LIKES TO BE CALLED.

DID YOU STILL DREAM OF 1963, AND WHAT MIGHT HAVE BEEN?

LAST EVENING AT HIGHBURY IT ALL ENDED THE SAME WAY.

YOU'VE SPILLED A LOT OF BLOOD FOR BRITAIN, 'ENRY. HERE'S HOPING WE SEE MUCH, MUCH MORE OF YOU.

BOB BOND – ILLUSTRATOR

Bob Bond, a lifelong Preston North End fan, was born in Lancashire and grew up always wanting to illustrate Western comics, Cowboys and Indians! But the first stories he was commissioned to draw for were football related.

"There's a World Cup coming," they said. "Can you draw footballers?"

And so Bob did. Very well.

His earliest pages were for Valiant and Tiger comics and then Scorcher and Football Monthly.

Bob's first child was born on July 11 1966 – the opening day of the World Cup at Wembley. So, having held his new-born son and kissed his exhausted wife, he drove home in a daze just in time to get his pencils out and start drawing.

The results are in this book.

Incidentally, his 1966 son, Philip, grew up to become an artist like his dad and is now illustrating comics in America for DC and Marvel.